defining twilight

defining twilight

Vocabulary Workbook for Unlocking the *SAT, ACT®, GED®, and SSAT®

Brian Leaf, M.A.

WILEY

Wiley Publishing, Inc.

Library of Congress Cataloging-in-Publication Data:
Leaf, Brian.
    Defining Twilight : vocabulary workbook for unlocking the SAT, ACT, GED, and SSAT / by Brian Leaf.
      p. cm.
    ISBN-13: 978-0-470-50743-8
    ISBN-10: 0-470-50743-8
    1. Vocabulary tests--Study guides. 2. Vocabulary--Study and teaching (Secondary) 3. Educational tests and measurements--Study guides. 4. Meyer, Stephenie, 1973- Twilight. I. Title. II. Title: Vocabulary workbook for unlocking the SAT, ACT, GED, and SSAT.
    PE1449.L32 2009
    428.1'076--dc22
                                                2009018186

Printed in the United States of America

10 9 8 7 6 5 4 3 2 1

Book production by Wiley Publishing, Inc., Composition Services

Acknowledgments

Thanks to Stephenie Meyer for her storytelling and her terrific vocabulary. Thanks to my agent, Linda Roghaar, and my fantastic editors at Wiley, Greg Tubach and Carol Pogoni. Thanks to Amy Sell, Malati Chavali, and Adrienne Fontaine at Wiley for getting the word out. Thanks to Pam Weber-Leaf for great editing tips, Zach Nelson for sage marketing advice, Ian Curtis for assiduous proofreading, Manny and Susan Leaf for everything, and of course, thanks most of all to Gwen and Noah for love, support, and inspiration.

Table of Contents

About the Author

Brian Leaf, M.A., is the author of the four-book SAT and ACT test-prep series *McGraw-Hill's Top 50 Skills*. He is Director of the New Leaf Learning Center in Massachusetts, and has provided SAT, ACT, GED, SSAT, and GRE preparation to thousands of students throughout the United States. Brian also works with the Georgetown University Office of Undergraduate Admissions as an alumni interviewer, and is a certified yoga instructor and avid meditator. For more information, visit his Web site at www.brianleaf.com.

How to Use This Book

This workbook contains 40 groups of vocabulary words selected from *Twilight*. Many of these words will show up on your SAT, ACT, GED, or SSAT. Beginning at Group 1, refer to the *Twilight* page where each vocabulary word appears. Read the word in context and come up with a definition. Then check your definitions against those provided in this workbook and make corrections. I'll also show you synonyms, word parts, and memorization tools. Read these over a few times, and then complete the drills. Do that for all 40 groups. There's no easier or more fun way to learn 600 vocabulary words! By the end of this book, your vocabulary will be larger, your test scores will be higher, and you'll be a *Twilight* scholar!

Noble Death?

Find each of the following words on the *Twilight* page number provided. Based on the way each word is used in the book, guess at its definition.

1. **Noble** (p. 1) might mean _____

_____

2. **Sauntered** (p. 1) might mean _____

_____

3. **Inconsequential** (p. 3) might mean _____

_____

4. **Omnipresent** (p. 3) might mean _____

_____

5. **Exiled** (p. 4) might mean _____

_____

6. **Detested** (p. 4) might mean _____

_____

7. **Erratic** (p. 4) might mean _____

_____

8. **Permanence** (p. 5) might mean _____

_____

2 Let's see how you did. Check your answers, write the exact definitions, and reread the sentences in *Twilight* where each word appears. Then complete the drills on the next page.

1. **Noble** (p. 1) means *dignified* or *honorable,* like a king . . . or a "vegetarian" vampire.

2. **Sauntered** (p. 1) means *walked in a slow and leisurely manner.* The word even sounds slow and relaxed.

3. **Inconsequential** (p. 3) means *not important.* This is a cool word to break apart. *In-* means *not,* as in *inconsistent* or *ineffective,* and *consequential* means *having consequences.* That's why *inconsequential* means *not having consequences—unimportant.*

4. **Omnipresent** (p. 3) means *present in all places* or *common.* This is another great word to break apart. *Omni-* means *all* or *everywhere,* as in *omnipotent,* which means *all powerful.* Synonym: ubiquitous.

5. **Exiled** (p. 4) means *sent away* or *banished.* Pretty much anytime you see a word that starts with *ex-,* it has to do with being released or going away, as in *exit, excursion, ex-boyfriend,* and *exception.*

6. **Detested** (p. 4) means *hated a lot.* You could say that Edward detested James, though even that is an understatement.

7. **Erratic** (p. 4) means *inconsistent* or *unpredictable.* Synonyms: arbitrary, capricious, fickle, impetuous, sporadic, whimsical.

8. **Permanence** (p. 5) means *lastingness* or *the state of remaining the same.* Synonyms: eternalness, intransience. You can see that *permanence* means *lastingness* by reading the sentence that follows it in *Twilight*—Charlie registered Bella for school, so she must be staying for a while. Using context is a great skill for the SAT, ACT, GED, SSAT, or any standardized test.

Synonyms: Select the word or phrase whose meaning is closest to the word in capital letters.

1. NOBLE
    A. inconsequential
    B. omnipresent
    C. permanent
    D. regal
    E. intransient

2. SAUNTER
    A. detest
    B. amble
    C. fly
    D. run
    E. rush

3. UBIQUITOUS
    A. all-present
    B. exiled
    C. irregular
    D. inconsequential
    E. relaxed

4. DETEST
    A. love
    B. regret
    C. hate
    D. lament
    E. respect

Analogies: Select the answer choice that best completes the meaning of the sentence.

5. Inconsequential is to insignificant as
    A. saunter is to run
    B. exile is to welcome
    C. permanence is to stability
    D. noble is to indecent
    E. omnipresent is to hateful

6. Banished is to hailed as
    A. eternal is to permanent
    B. omnipotent is to feeble
    C. hated is to detested
    D. erratic is to pale
    E. noble is to honorable

Sentence Completions: Choose the word or phrase that, when inserted in the sentence, <u>best</u> fits the meaning of the sentence as a whole.

7. Katie _____ vampires, she feared and hated them and wrongly assumed that all were out to get her.
    A. comprehended
    B. appreciated
    C. preferred
    D. detested
    E. sought out

8. Si-Shen had grown to expect Jon's erratic and _____ mood swings.
    A. noble
    B. capricious
    C. permanent
    D. ubiquitous
    E. exiled

1. **D.** *Noble* means *dignified* or *royal*. The best answer is *regal*, which means *royal*. *Inconsequential* means *not important*, *omnipresent* means *present everywhere*, *permanent* means *lasting*, and *intransient* also means *lasting* (*in-* means *not*, and *trans-* means *across*, so *intransient* means *not across*, or *staying put—lasting!*).

2. **B.** *Saunter* means *stroll*. Use the process of elimination—cross out all choices that are **definitely** wrong. *Amble* also means *stroll* and is the best answer.

3. **A.** *Ubiquitous* means *present everywhere* or *all-present*, just like *omnipresent*.

4. **C.** *Detest* means *hate*. It's the opposite of love and respect. *Lament* means *regret* and is a bit closer, but choice C is certainly the best answer.

5. **C.** Make a sentence with the two words. For example, "Inconsequential means insignificant." Then, try your sentence for each pair of words.
   - A. Saunter (stroll) means run . . . no.
   - B. Exile (send away) means welcome . . . no.
   - (C.) Permanence means stability . . . yep, *permanence* means *staying the same*.
   - D. Noble means indecent . . . no, it means the opposite.
   - E. Omnipresent (present everywhere) means hateful . . . no way, they are totally unrelated.

6. **B.** "Banished (sent away) is the opposite of hailed (called for— Angela *hailed* a cab in Seattle)."
   - A. Eternal is the opposite of permanent . . . no, they are synonyms.
   - (B.) Omnipotent (all powerful) is the opposite of feeble (weak) . . . yes!
   - C. Hated is the opposite of detested . . . no, they are synonyms.
   - D. Erratic (inconsistent) is the opposite of pale . . . no, they are totally unrelated.
   - E. Noble is the opposite of honorable . . . no, they are synonyms.

7. **D.** Think of a word to fill the blank. Often you can borrow a word right out of the sentence. Then see which answer choice fits best:

   "Katie *feared/hated* vampires, she feared and hated them and wrongly assumed that all were out to get her."

   Use the process of elimination. Cross off answer choices that definitely do not work. You want a negative word, like "feared" or "hated." Only choice D (*detested*) works.

8. **B.** "Si-Shen had grown to expect Jon's erratic and *erratic* mood swings."
   When trying to come up with a word to fill the blank, always look for evidence in the sentence. The words "erratic" and "mood swings" tell you what you need. *Capricious* works best; it is a synonym for *erratic* and refers to *sudden and unexpected changes*.

A Pallid Reflection

Find each of the following words on the *Twilight* page number provided. Based on the way each word is used in the book, guess at its definition.

1. **Verbose** (p. 5) might mean _____

   _____

2. **Permeable** (p. 6) might mean _____

   _____

3. **Supplement** (p. 6) might mean _____

   _____

4. **Bulbous** (p. 8) might mean _____

   _____

5. **Stipulation** (p. 9) might mean _____

   _____

6. **Communal** (p. 10) might mean _____

   _____

7. **Translucent** (p. 10) might mean _____

   _____

8. **Pallid** (p. 10) might mean _____

   _____

Let's see how you did. Check your answers, write the exact definitions, and reread the sentence in *Twilight* where each word appears. Then complete the drills.

1. **Verbose** (p. 5) means *wordy*, like a friend or teacher who talks too much. Basically, anytime you see *verb* in a word, it will have to do with words. That's why *verbal* means *pertaining to words*, and *verbatim* means *word for word*.

2. **Permeable** (p. 6) means *allowing liquids to pass through*. And, since the prefix *im-* means *not*, **im**permeable means **not** *allowing liquids to pass through*. In fact, *impermeable* means raincoat in French!

3. **Supplement** (p. 6) means *add something that completes*. That's why the vitamins that you take (for *complete* nutrition) are called supplements.

4. **Bulbous** (p. 8) means *rounded* or *bulging*. That's easy to remember since *bulbous* basically means *shaped like a bulb*.

5. **Stipulation** (p. 9) means *a requirement*, usually in a bargain. This word has a bizarre special use in professional wrestling, where the agreement before a match might *stipulate* that the loser is required to leave town, retire, or shave his or her head.

6. **Communal** (p. 10) means *shared*. The prefix *com-* means *with* or *together*. That makes sense for the words *community* (a group together), *communication* (interacting together), and *compilation* (songs grouped together). You can even use this prefix to get a challenging SAT word like *compendious*, which means *presenting lots of information together in one place*, like in a book.

7. **Translucent** (p. 10) means *semi-transparent*, like frosted glass. This is a cool word to break apart. *Trans-* means *through* or *across*, *luc* implies *light* (like *luz* in Spanish), and *-ent* can mean *occurrence*. That's why *translucent* means *the occurrence of light going through!*

8. **Pallid** (p. 10) means *pale*. A vampire's pale white skin is *pallid*. Enough said!

Synonyms: Select the word or phrase whose meaning is closest to the word in capital letters.

1. BULBOUS
   A. shared
   B. transparent
   C. rounded
   D. stipulated
   E. lucid

2. PALLOR
   A. noble behavior
   B. compendious
   C. pale appearance
   D. omnipresent
   E. lucidity

3. VERBATIM
   A. sprawled
   B. literally
   C. erratically
   D. genuinely
   E. permissive

4. PERMEABLE
   A. supplementary
   B. vigorous
   C. harebrained
   D. inconsequential
   E. leaky

Analogies: Select the answer choice that best completes the meaning of the sentence.

5. Stipulate is to demand as
   A. supplement is to add
   B. transpire is to elucidate
   C. agree is to dispute
   D. pallid is to vampire
   E. commune is to solo

6. Verbose is to brief as
   A. compelled is to suspicious
   B. transparent is to translucent
   C. bulbous is to flat
   D. verbal is to spoken
   E. permissive is to unstipulated

Sentence Completions: Choose the word that, when inserted in the sentence, best fits the meaning of the sentence as a whole.

7. Some of the articles found in academic journals are characterized by _____ language and could be made much shorter.
   A. brief
   B. verbose
   C. supplementary
   D. omniscient
   E. compelling

8. Simone was nauseous, and her face had such a _____ tone that the nurse decided to send her home.
   A. pallid
   B. opaque
   C. compendious
   D. transcending
   E. vigorous

1. **C.** *Bulbous* means *rounded.*

2. **C.** *Pallor* means *a pale appearance,* like that of a vampire. Group 1 told you that choice A, *noble,* means *royal* or *of high principles,* and yes, a vampire might be noble, but that's too much of a leap of logic to be the right answer. Also, recall from Group 1 that *omnipresent* means *very widespread.*

3. **B.** *Verbatim* means *word for word* or *exactly.* That's also what *literally* means. In fact, the Latin word *littera* means *letter,* which is awfully close to *word,* the meaning of the Latin *verbum.*

4. **E.** *Permeable* means *allowing liquid through,* so *leaky* is the best choice. *Vigorous* means *energetic,* and *inconsequential* means *not consequential* or *not meaningful.*

5. **A.** Make a sentence with the two words. For example, "When you stipulate, you demand something." Then, try your sentence for each pair of words.

   (A.) When you supplement, you add something . . . yes!

   B . When you transpire, you elucidate something . . . no, **trans**pire means *occur* or *water flowing **through** the stoma of a plant,* and *elucidate* means *shed **light** on* or *explain.*

   C . When you agree, you dispute something . . . no.

   D . When you pallid, you vampire something . . . no way, vampires are pale, but this sentence makes no sense!

   E . When you commune (join together), you solo something . . . no, the opposite.

6. **C.** "Verbose is the opposite of brief."

   A . Compelled (forced) is the opposite of suspicious . . . no.

   B . Transparent is the opposite of translucent . . . no, they are slightly different, but not opposites.

   (C.) Bulbous is the opposite of flat . . . yes!

   D . Verbal is the opposite of spoken . . . no.

   E . Permissive (lenient) is the opposite of unstipulated (unrequired) . . . no.

7. **B.** Think of a word to fill the blank and then see which answer choice fits best:

   > "Some of the articles found in academic journals are character- ized by _not short_ language and could be made much shorter."

   Verbose means *wordy* or *not short. Compelling* means *convincing* and might seem to fit, but does not relate to "be made much shorter."

8. **A.** "Simone was nauseous, and her face had such a _nauseous/pale_ tone that the nurse decided to send her home."

   Choice A, *pallid,* means *pale* and works best. *Opaque* means *solid, compendious* means *presenting lots of information together in one place,* and *transcending* means *going beyond.*

A Precarious Niche

Find each of the following words on the *Twilight* page number provided. Based on the way each word is used in the book, guess at its definition.

1. **Niche** (p. 10) might mean _____

   _____

2. **Claustrophobia** (p. 11) might mean _____

   _____

3. **Donned** (p. 12) might mean _____

   _____

4. **Eaves** (p. 12) might mean _____

   _____

5. **Nostalgically** (p. 13) might mean _____

   _____

6. **Commercial** (p. 13) might mean _____

   _____

7. **Precariously** (p. 14) might mean _____

   _____

8. **Hyperventilation** (p. 15) might mean _____

   _____

Let's see how you did. Check your answers, write the exact definitions, and reread the sentence in *Twilight* where each word appears. Then complete the drills.

1. **Niche** (p. 10) means *a comfortable or appropriate position,* like a group of friends who also do Wii Fit yoga everyday after school.

2. **Claustrophobia** (p. 11) means *fear of confined spaces.* Any time you see the ending *-phobia,* it's a "fear" word:

   Arachnophobia—fear of spiders (*arachno-* refers to *spiders*)

   Aerophobia—fear of flying (*aero-* means *air*)

   Emetophobia—fear of vomit (*Emet-* is like *emit* which means *discharge,* or basically puke)

   Necrophobia—fear of death (*necro-* means *death*)

3. **Donned** (p. 12) means *put on (usually clothes).*

4. **Eaves** (p. 12) is *the part of a roof that hangs over the side of a house.* The word *eavesdrop,* which means *to covertly listen to a conversation,* comes from people skulking near the side of a house in order to listen in on conversations.

5. **Nostalgically** (p. 13) means *longingly remembering the past.* Synonym: wistfully.

6. **Commercial** (p. 13) in this case means *industrial. Commercial* can also refer to a *television advertisement,* or mean *business-related.* This is great practice—standardized tests love to see if you can determine how a word with several meanings is used in a reading passage.

7. **Precariously** (p. 14) means *unsteadily,* like something about to topple. Synonym: perilously.

8. **Hyperventilation** (p. 15) means *breathing overly fast.* This is a terrific word to break apart: *hyper-* means *over* (like *hyperactive* means *overactive*) and *ventilate* means *cause air to flow,* as in the heating *vents* at your school.

Synonyms: Select the word or phrase whose meaning is closest to the word in capital letters.

1. DON
   A. wistful
   B. commercial
   C. a small man
   D. to stroll
   E. to dress

2. PERILOUS
   A. dangerous
   B. suspicious
   C. pale
   D. omnipresent
   E. clear

3. NICHE
   A. omen
   B. sprawl
   C. appropriate position
   D. fear of snakes
   E. verbosity

4. WISTFUL
   A. automatic
   B. genuine
   C. erratic
   D. inconsequential
   E. nostalgic

Analogies: Select the answer choice that best completes the meaning of the sentence.

5. Eaves is to roof as
   A. cuff is to shirt
   B. pants are to donned
   C. niche is to nook
   D. pale is to vampire
   E. exile is to home

6. Hyperventilate is to breathe as
   A. verbose is to quiet
   B. erratic is to constant
   C. detest is to dislike
   D. verbal is to spoken
   E. bulbous is to flat

Sentence Completions: Choose the word or words that, when inserted in the sentence, <u>best</u> fits the meaning of the sentence as a whole.

7. Clara had none of her sister's _____; she was neither homesick nor reflective.
   A. nobility
   B. verbosity
   C. claustrophobia
   D. donning
   E. wistfulness

8. Maria was standing _____ close to the edge of the cliff; clearly she had overcome her previous _____.
   A. perilously . . acrophobia
   B. precariously . . claustrophobia
   C. nostalgically . . stipulation
   D. dangerously . . niche
   E. suspiciously . . arachnophobia

1. **E.** *Don* means *to put on* or *to dress,* as in to get dressed for school.

2. **A.** *Perilous* means *risky* or *dangerous.* You might be *suspicious* (choice B) of a perilous situation, but the correct synonym should be more directly connected.

3. **C.** *Niche* means *an appropriate position.* An *omen* is *a sign* or *a warning,* like your boyfriend skipping Biology class on the day when students prick their fingers to determine blood type.

4. **E.** *Wistful* means *longingly remembering the past* or *nostalgic.*

5. **A.** "Eaves are the edge of a roof."
   - A. Cuff is the edge of a shirt . . . yes!
   - B. Pants are the edge of a donned . . . rubbish! That makes no sense.
   - C. Niche is the edge of a nook . . . no, they are synonyms, so it makes no sense.
   - D. Pale is the edge of a vampire . . . no way! Don't over-think this one and somehow convince yourself that pale is the edge of a vampire. If it takes more than one short sentence to describe the connection, then it doesn't work.
   - E. Exile is the edge of a home . . . no, *exile* is *being away from or leaving home,* but it's not the edge of home.

6. **C.** "Hyperventilate means breathe a lot."
   - A. Verbose means quiet a lot . . . no, verbose means the opposite of quiet.
   - B. Erratic means constant a lot . . . no, erratic means the opposite of constant.
   - C. Detest means dislike a lot . . . yes, *detest* means *hate!*
   - D. Verbal means spoken a lot . . . close, but it doesn't really make sense. *Verbal* means *pertaining to words* or *spoken,* but nothing about *a lot.*
   - E. Bulbous means flat a lot . . . no, sir, they are opposites.

7. **E.** "Clara had none of her sister's *homesickness;* she was neither homesick nor reflective."

   You want a word for *homesickness. Wistfulness* means *longing* and works best.

8. **A.** "Maria was standing *very* close to the edge of the cliff; clearly she had overcome her previous *fear.*"

   Think of a word to fill each blank and use the process of elimination for one blank and then the other. Only cross out choices that **definitely** do not fit. If a word could work or if you're not sure, leave it. Choice A is best—*perilously* means *dangerously* and *acrophobia* means *fear of heights.* Even if you didn't know *acrophobia,* you could get this one with the process of elimination!

Apprehensive Stammering

Find each of the following words on the *Twilight* page number provided. Based on the way each word is used in the book, guess at its definition.

1. **Gawked** (p. 15) might mean _____

   _____

2. **Droned** (p. 15) might mean _____

   _____

3. **Apprehensively** (p. 16) might mean _____

   _____

4. **Stammered** (p. 17) might mean _____

   _____

5. **Prattled** (p. 17) might mean _____

   _____

6. **Statuesque** (p. 18) might mean _____

   _____

7. **Lithe** (p. 19) might mean _____

   _____

8. **Vogue** (p. 20) might mean _____

   _____

Let's see how you did. Check your answers, write the exact definitions, and reread the sentence in *Twilight* where each word appears. Then complete the drills.

1. **Gawked** (p. 15) means *stared stupidly*. This was not a compliment to Bella's teacher. It means he had an empty stare and looked dull. Synonym: gaped.

2. **Droned** (p. 15) means *spoke in a dull, monotonous tone*. Not a lot of love for this teacher; but, I guess we've all had a few teachers like him. You should check out the classic movie *Ferris Bueller's Day Off* for a good example of a droning teacher. By the way, *monotonous* is an interesting word to break apart. *Mono-* means *one* (like *monochromatic* means *one color*), and *ton* is like *tone*, referring to *sound*; so *monotonous* means *only one sound*—boring!

3. **Apprehensively** (p. 16) means *uneasily* or even *anxiously*.

4. **Stammered** (p. 17) means *stuttered* or *stumbled with words*.

5. **Prattled** (p. 17) means *chattered* or even *babbled*. A person prattling is probably speaking with more excitement than someone who is droning. And a person who prattles is definitely verbose, like Jessica when she talks about Mike.

6. **Statuesque** (p. 18) means *attractively tall and imposing*, like the statue of a Greek goddess.

7. **Lithe** (p. 19) means *flexible and graceful*, like a dancer or a gazelle. Synonyms: agile, lissome, nimble, supple.

8. **Vogue** (p. 20) means *the popular fashion or style*, as in *Vogue*® magazine or Madonna's song "Vogue."

Synonyms: Select the word or phrase whose meaning is closest to the word in capital letters.

1. DRONE
   A. speak tediously
   B. queen bee
   C. chatter
   D. stipulate
   E. eavesdrop

2. LITHE
   A. noble behavior
   B. compendious
   C. gazelle-like
   D. nostalgic
   E. bulbous

3. STAMMERED
   A. sprawled
   B. prattled
   C. stumbled
   D. hyperventilated
   E. gawked

4. STATUESQUE
   A. supplementary
   B. permeable
   C. noble
   D. exiled
   E. attractive and stately

Analogies: Select the answer choice that best completes the meaning of the sentence.

5. Queen is to noble as
   A. dancer is to lithe
   B. teacher is to apprehensive
   C. choreographer is to claustrophobic
   D. baker is to permeable
   E. conductor is to verbose

6. Prattled is to erratic as
   A. listened is to constant
   B. stipulated is to unpredictable
   C. gawked is to flat
   D. sauntered is to verbal
   E. supplemented is to literal

Sentence Completions: Choose the word that, when inserted in the sentence, best fits the meaning of the sentence as a whole.

7. The dancer was known for his _____ movements; his deft performance exhibited strength, flexibility, and grace.
   A. stammering
   B. lithe
   C. vogue
   D. gawking
   E. erratic

8. The new teacher droned on and on about the _____ of consumers during the Great Depression of the early 1900s.
   A. nimbleness
   B. opacity
   C. stipulation
   D. apprehension
   E. permeability

1. **A.** *Drone* means *speak in a dull, monotonous tone.* That's also what *speak tediously* means. Don't be confused by choice B; a drone can be a male bee, but not the queen. And choice C, *chatter,* is about talking, but not necessarily monotonously.

2. **C.** *Lithe* means *flexible* and *graceful,* like a gazelle. *Noble* means *dignified, compendious* means *concise but complete, nostalgic* means *longing for home,* and *bulbous* means *rounded,* like a bulb.

3. **C.** *Stammered* means *stumbled with words.* Watch out for choice A, *sprawled.* If Bella stumbles, she might wind up sprawled out on the ground, but that's too much of a leap from stammer to stumble to sprawl. The correct answer will always be pretty direct. If you need to use several sentences to explain the link, then it is not the correct answer.

4. **E.** *Statuesque* means *attractive and dignified* or *stately.* Make sure you try all of the choices. Don't just get to a decent answer and stop. Choice C, *noble,* almost works, but choice E is certainly the best answer. Always try all choices and use the process of elimination to find the **best** one.

5. **A.** "A good queen is noble."
   A. A good dancer is lithe . . . yes, a good dancer is graceful.
   B. A good teacher is apprehensive . . . no, a good teacher is not necessarily worried.
   C. A good choreographer is claustrophobic . . . no, a good dance designer is not necessarily afraid of confined spaces.
   D. A good baker is permeable . . . no way, a good baker is probably not leaky!
   E. A good conductor is verbose . . . no, a good conductor is not necessarily very talkative.

6. **A.** This setup is very interesting. Usually the two words in the analogy are directly related to each other, and the best strategy is to make a sentence that defines one with the other. However, occasionally on the SSAT, the two words are related not to each other but to the two words below. You can recognize this setup when the words in the question are totally unrelated. In that case, set up a relationship to the words below. Choice A is correct since *prattled* is the opposite of *listen,* and *erratic* is the opposite of *constant.*

7. **B.** "The dancer was known for his *deft/graceful* movements; his deft performance exhibited strength, flexibility, and grace."
   Use the process of elimination. *Lithe* means *graceful.*

8. **D.** "The new teacher droned on and on about the *problems/depression* of consumers during the Great Depression of the early 1900s."
   Choice D, *apprehension,* means *anxiety* and works best.

Surreptitious Glances

Find each of the following words on the *Twilight* page number provided. Based on the way each word is used in the book, guess at its definition.

1. **Condemnation** (p. 20) might mean _____

   _____

2. **Surreptitiously** (p. 23) might mean _____

   _____

3. **Hostile** (p. 23) might mean _____

   _____

4. **Antagonistic** (p. 23) might mean _____

   _____

5. **Averting** (p. 23) might mean _____

   _____

6. **Inconspicuously** (p. 23) might mean _____

   _____

7. **Burly** (p. 24) might mean _____

   _____

8. **Mandatory** (p. 26) might mean _____

   _____

Let's see how you did. Check your answers, write the exact definitions, and reread the sentence in *Twilight* where each word appears. Then complete the drills.

1. **Condemnation** (p. 20) means *strong disapproval.* Synonyms for *condemn:* censure, denounce, rebuke, reproach (less strong disapproval), reprove. *Very malicious (mean) condemnation* is called *vituperative.* That word even sounds mean—my face tightens as I say it.

2. **Surreptitiously** (p. 23) means *secretly.* Synonyms: clandestinely, covertly, furtively.

3. **Hostile** (p. 23) means *very unfriendly.* FYI, this paragraph in *Twilight* is where it all begins . . .

4. **Antagonistic** (p. 23) means *hostile.* Let's see this word in context. ". . . the *antagonistic* (italics added) stare he'd given me" refers back to Edward's *hostile, furious* expression, and that's the definition of antagonistic! The SAT, ACT, GED, and SSAT do this, too; so if you're not sure of the meaning of a word in a reading comprehension question, look at the context!

5. **Averting** (p. 23) means *turning away.* I love the scene in *Monty Python and the Holy Grail* where King Arthur says, "I am averting my eyes, oh Lord." (Twentieth Century Fox, 1975) Check it out.

6. **Inconspicuously** (p. 23) means *not conspicuously* or *discreetly.* As you've seen before, *in-* means *not,* like *inattentive* means *not attentive. Inconspicuously* is a bit like *surreptitiously,* but whereas *inconspicuous* means *discreet, surreptitious* means *secret.*

7. **Burly** (p. 24) means *large and muscular.* Emmett is the definition of burly.

8. **Mandatory** (p. 26) means *required.* When you notice an English word that reminds you of a Spanish or French word, they are usually related. *Mandatory* looks a lot like the Spanish word *mandato,* which means *command.* Using knowledge of another language, such as Spanish, French, Latin, or German, is a great way to feel out the definitions of new words. Synonyms: compulsory, obligatory (like the word *obligation*), requisite.

Synonyms: Select the word or phrase whose meaning is closest to the word in capital letters.

1. CONDEMN
   A. reprove
   B. avert
   C. stipulate
   D. appreciate
   E. don

2. CONSPICUOUS
   A. consequential
   B. compendious
   C. obvious
   D. noble
   E. communal

3. ANTAGONISTIC
   A. hasty
   B. bulbous
   C. erratic
   D. hostile
   E. permissive

4. BURLY
   A. precarious
   B. vigorous
   C. hefty
   D. nostalgic
   E. erratic

Analogies: Select the answer choice that best completes the meaning of the sentence.

5. Inconspicuous is to surreptitious as
   A. precarious is to steady
   B. apprehensive is to relaxed
   C. permeable is to water
   D. stipulation is to option
   E. prattle is to chatter

6. Stipulation is to mandatory as
   A. permanence is to lasting
   B. sofa is to translucent
   C. supplement is to erratic
   D. condemnation is to verbose
   E. permission is to unstipulated

Sentence Completions: Choose the word or phrase that, when inserted in the sentence, best fits the meaning of the sentence as a whole.

7. In many states, physical education class is a _____ part of high school curriculum, and students are required to complete a certain number of credits.
   A. surreptitious
   B. verbose
   C. compulsory
   D. burly
   E. whimsical

8. The governor felt obligated to _____ the state senator for his unprofessional conduct and erratic attendance at senate meetings.
   A. gawk at
   B. censure
   C. stammer at
   D. exile
   E. antagonize

1. **A.** *Condemn* and *reprove* both mean *criticize.* Let's see if you remember the rest of the choices. *Avert* means *turn away, stipulate* means *require, appreciate* means *be grateful for,* and *don* means *put on (clothes).*

2. **C.** *Conspicuous* means *obvious. Consequential* means *important, compendious* means *concise, noble* means *dignified,* and *communal* means *shared.*

3. **D.** *Antagonistic* and *hostile* both mean *unfriendly. Hasty* means *rushed, bulbous* means *rounded, erratic* means *unpredictable,* and *permissive* means *lenient.*

4. **C.** *Burly* and *hefty* both mean *large and stocky.* Remember to use the process of elimination—cross off answers that **definitely** don't work and choose the best of what's left. *Precarious* means *unstable, vigorous* means *energetic, nostalgic* means *homesick,* and *erratic* means *unpredictable.*

5. **E.** "Inconspicuous and surreptitious are synonyms."
   A. Precarious and steady are synonyms . . . no, opposites.
   B. Apprehensive and relaxed are synonyms . . . no, opposites.
   C. Permeable and water are synonyms . . . no, *permeable* means *water can flow through.*
   D. Stipulation and option are synonyms . . . no, a *stipulation* is a *requirement,* not an *option.*
   E. Prattle and chatter are synonyms . . . yes, they both mean *talk a lot.*

6. **A.** "A stipulation is mandatory."
   A. A permanence is lasting . . . yes!
   B. A sofa is translucent (allowing light through) . . . no, although that would be one cool sofa.
   C. A supplement is erratic . . . no.
   D. A condemnation is verbose . . . no, a strong criticism could be wordy or brief.
   E. A permission is unstipulated . . . no, if you think about it, this actually makes no sense.

7. **C.** "In many states, physical education class is a _required_ part of high school curriculum, and students are required to complete a certain number of credits."
   Compulsory means *required.* Watch out for choice D; going to the gym might make you burly, but the class itself is not burly.

8. **B.** "The governor felt obligated to _criticize_ the state senator for his unprofessional conduct and erratic attendance at senate meetings."
   Censure means *criticize publicly. Exile* means *send away,* and almost works, but is a bit too harsh for the sentence. The senator will be criticized, but not likely exiled to Siberia.

Quiz 1

I. Let's review some of the words that you've seen in Groups 1–5. Match each of the following words to the correct definition or synonym on the right. Then check the solutions on page 171.

1. Noble
2. Inconsequential
3. Omnipresent
4. Detest
5. Erratic
6. Intransience
7. Verbose
8. Supplement
9. Compendious
10. Wistful
11. Precarious
12. Lithe
13. Condemn
14. Surreptitious
15. Requisite

A. Secret
B. Mandatory
C. Hate
D. Wordy
E. Nostalgic
F. Graceful
G. Dignified
H. Unimportant
I. Capricious
J. Criticize
K. Dangerous
L. Concise but complete
M. Permanence
N. Ubiquitous
O. Add on to complete

II. Let's review several of the word parts that you've seen in Groups 1–5. Match each of the following word parts to the correct definition or synonym on the right. Then check the solutions on page 171.

16. Omni-
17. In-, Im-
18. Com-
19. Phobia-
20. Trans-
21. Hyper-

A. Through or across
B. With or together
C. Fear
D. All or everywhere
E. Not
F. Over or very

Tousled Hair

Find each of the following words on the *Twilight* page number provided. Based on the way each word is used in the book, guess at its definition.

1. **Literally** (p. 26) might mean _____
   _____

2. **Tousled** (p. 26) might mean _____
   _____

3. **Hastily** (p. 27) might mean _____
   _____

4. **Maternally** (p. 27) might mean _____
   _____

5. **Haven** (p. 28) might mean _____
   _____

6. **Opaque** (p. 29) might mean _____
   _____

7. **Terminator** (p. 30) might mean _____
   _____

8. **Elated** (p. 30) might mean _____
   _____

and reread the sentence in *Twilight* where each word appears. Then complete the drills.

1. **Literally** (p. 26) means *factually* or *exactly*. Remember from Group 2 that *literally*, like *verbatim*, has to do with words being exact. Sometimes *literally* is used when something is actually true and sometimes it is used (as on page 26 in *Twilight*) to give strong emphasis.

2. **Tousled** (p. 26) means *messy*, usually for hair.

3. **Hastily** (p. 27) means *hurriedly*. If you've ever played Dungeons & Dragons, or dated anyone who played Dungeons & Dragons, you might know that Haste is a third-level spell that makes you move really fast.

4. **Maternally** (p. 27) means *related to or like a mother*. It can also mean *on your mother's side*—as in your maternal grandma.

5. **Haven** (p. 28) means *place of safety or comfort*. It sounds a lot like *heaven*, which is a great way to remember it, though it is actually unrelated. *Haven* comes from the German word for harbor, since a harbor represents a **place of safety** for boats.

6. **Opaque** (p. 29) means *solid* or *unclear* or *not transparent*—basically something that you can't see through. Figuratively, it can also mean *a difficult or unclear concept that is hard to grasp*. Notice that this word is basically defined in the sentence that it appears in— " . . . the clouds were dense and *opaque*." Dense is very similar to opaque. The SAT, ACT, GED, and SSAT always do that, too; you can figure out the general meaning of a word from the words around it.

7. **Terminator** (p. 30) means *one who terminates or kills*, like Arnold Schwarzenegger in *The Terminator* (or Shermanator in *American Pie*!).

8. **Elated** (p. 30) means *very psyched*. Synonyms: ecstatic, euphoric, jubilant, rapturous.

Synonyms: Select the word or phrase whose meaning is closest to the word in capital letters.

1. MATERNAL
   A. shared
   B. avuncular
   C. aged
   D. motherly
   E. statuesque

2. OPAQUE
   A. translucent
   B. transparent
   C. elated
   D. open
   E. solid

3. HAVEN
   A. exile
   B. community
   C. refuge
   D. supplement
   E. skirmish

4. ECSTATIC
   A. hyperaware
   B. euphoric
   C. hostile
   D. morose
   E. sad

Analogies: Select the answer choice that best completes the meaning of the sentence.

5. Wind is to tousle as
   A. brick is to construct
   B. storm is to tempest
   C. judge is to condemn
   D. vampire is to play baseball
   E. frog is to avert

6. Spy is to surreptitious as
   A. friend is to antagonistic
   B. enemy is to hostile
   C. stuntperson is to perilous
   D. dancer is to capricious
   E. king is to exiled

Sentence Completions: Choose the word or words that, when inserted in the sentence, <u>best</u> fits the meaning of the sentence as a whole.

7. Amit considered his mother's house to be a _____ from his hectic life, and referred to it as the _____ sanctuary.
   A. elation .. literal
   B. tousled .. opaque
   C. haven .. maternal
   D. hostile .. inconspicuous
   E. nostalgia .. commercial

8. Sonja was _____ when she received the news that she had won a full college scholarship.
   A. elated
   B. terminated
   C. literal
   D. hasty
   E. reproved

1. **D.** *Maternal* means *motherly* or *related to a mother.* I love the word in choice B, *avuncular,* which means *of or relating to an uncle.* It even sounds like "of uncle"!

2. **E.** *Opaque* means *solid*—no light passes through. *Elated* means *very happy.*

3. **C.** *Haven* means *place of safety* or *refuge.*

4. **B.** *Ecstatic* means *very psyched.* Let's use the process of elimination on the choices:
   A. Hyperaware means *very aware,* remember that *hyper-* means *very,* like *hyperactive.*
   (B.) Euphoric means *thrilled.*
   C. Hostile means *unfriendly.*
   D. Morose means *sad and sullen,* and is the opposite.
   E. Sad

5. **C.** "Wind might tousle (someone's hair)."
   A. Brick might construct . . . not bad, but a brick is **used** to construct, it does not do it.
   B. Storm might tempest . . . no, *tempest* is a *big storm.*
   (C.) Judge might condemn . . . yes, a judge might reprimand.
   D. A vampire might play baseball . . . they do like baseball and they might play, but this answer is not as definite as choice C.
   E. A frog might avert . . . now that's just crazy.

6. **B.** "A spy is surreptitious (sneaky)."
   A. A friend is antagonistic . . . no, a friend is not *antagonistic* (unfriendly).
   (B.) An enemy is hostile . . . yes, an enemy is probably *hostile* (unfriendly).
   C. A stuntperson is perilous . . . no, a stuntperson might do perilous things, but he or she is not *perilous* (dangerous).
   D. A dancer is capricious . . . no, a dancer is not necessarily erratic.
   E. A king is exiled . . . no, though many kings in history got booted, a king is not necessarily sent away.

7. **C.** "Amit considered his mother's house to be a _sanctuary_ from his hectic life, and referred to it as the _mother's house_ sanctuary."
   Use the process of elimination, one blank at a time. *Haven* means *sanctuary,* and *maternal* refers to *mother.*

8. **A.** "Sonja was _psyched_ when she received the news that she had won a full college scholarship." *Elated* is a terrific word for *psyched. Hasty* means *rushed,* and *reproved* means *scolded.*

Group 7
Subtle Hints

Find each of the following words on the *Twilight* page number provided. Based on the way each word is used in the book, guess at its definition.

1. **Wistfully** (p. 31) might mean _____

_____

2. **Diplomacy** (p. 31) might mean _____

_____

3. **Tactful** (p. 31) might mean _____

_____

4. **Egotistical** (p. 31) might mean _____

_____

5. **Evaded** (p. 31) might mean _____

_____

6. **Subtly** (p. 32) might mean _____

_____

7. **Warily** (p. 35) might mean _____

_____

8. **Lumbered** (p. 35) might mean _____

_____

and reread the sentence in *Twilight* where each word appears. Then complete the drills.

1. **Wistfully** (p. 31) means *reflectively* or *longingly*. Okay, here's the quiz. What word have you had that is basically a synonym for wistfully? Anyone? Anyone? Bueller? Yes, *nostalgically*.

2. **Diplomacy** (p. 31) means *dealing with people in a sensitive way*, i.e. not ticking them off. Synonyms: mediation, suave, tact.

3. **Tactful** (p. 31) means *full of tact*. It's basically a synonym for *diplomatic*. *Tact* is when you think twice before asking your teacher who recently gained a few pounds if she is pregnant.

4. **Egotistical** (p. 31) means *self-centered*. *Ego-* means *I* and *–ism* means *system* or *philosophy*, so *egotism* is *the philosophy of I— self-centeredness*. Synonyms: narcissistic, solipsistic, vain.

5. **Evaded** (p. 31) means *avoided*. Sometimes James Bond–type movies use the words *evasive action* or *evasive maneuvers*. Since *evasive* means *avoiding*, evasive maneuvers are maneuvers to avoid or escape from danger. Synonyms for *evade*: circumvent, elude, equivocate, prevaricate.

6. **Subtly** (p. 32) means *slightly, indirectly,* or *in a way that's understated*.

7. **Warily** (p. 35) means *cautiously*. Synonyms for *wary*: cagey, chary, circumspect, vigilant. *Circumspect* is a great ACT word. Let's break it apart. *Circum-* means *around,* as in *circumnavigate* (sail around), *circumvent* (go around—avoid), and the *circumference* of a circle; and *-spect* indicates *look,* as in *inspect* (look at—examine), *spectacles* (eyeglasses), and *spectacle* (something interesting to look at). So *circumspect* (looking around) means *cautious*.

8. **Lumbered** (p. 35) means *walked in a slow, awkward manner*. Imagine a giant, like Hagrid from the *Harry Potter* books, whose legs are as thick as tree trunks. He lumbers.

Synonyms: Select the word or phrase whose meaning is closest to the word in capital letters.

Drills

1. WISTFUL
   A. egotistical
   B. tactful
   C. hasty
   D. wary
   E. nostalgic

2. SUBTLE
   A. indirect
   B. verbose
   C. ubiquitous
   D. eternal
   E. fickle

3. WARY
   A. tactful
   B. circumspect
   C. tousled
   D. discreet
   E. burly

4. EVADE
   A. gawk
   B. prattle
   C. drone
   D. elude
   E. don

Analogies: Select the answer choice that best completes the meaning of the sentence.

5. Lithe is to lumber as
   A. wary is to worry
   B. evasive is to avoid
   C. egotistical is to boast
   D. diplomatic is to offend
   E. tactful is to mediate

6. Subtle is to obvious as
   A. vain is to modest
   B. transparent is to translucent
   C. bulbous is to bowed
   D. wistful is to longing
   E. elated is to euphoric

Sentence Completions: Choose the word that, when inserted in the sentence, best fits the meaning of the sentence as a whole.

7. Friends blame Joe's _____ philosophy for his selfish behavior.
   A. wistful
   B. suave
   C. tactful
   D. solipsistic
   E. circumspect

8. Mia avoided the agents who sought to capture her; she _____ them by entering the tunnels of the subway.
   A. lumbered
   B. terminated
   C. eluded
   D. tousled
   E. elated

1. **E.** *Wistful* and *nostalgic* mean *longing*. Let's review the others. *Egotistical* means *self-centered*, *tactful* means *diplomatic*, *hasty* means *rushed*, and *wary* means *cautious*.

2. **A.** *Subtle* means *not obvious* or *indirect*. *Verbose* means *wordy*, *ubiquitous* means *omnipresent* or *present everywhere*, *eternal* means *everlasting*, and *fickle* means *indecisive* or *erratic*.

3. **B.** *Wary* means *cautious*, which is exactly what *circumspect* (*spect*— looking, *circum*—all around) means. *Tactful* is the second best answer, but *tactful* means *careful about what one says*, though not in a wary or anxious way. Similarly, while someone being *discreet* might be wary of being caught, *wary* is not the meaning.

4. **D.** *Evade* means *avoid*, *avert*, or *elude*. Let's review the others. *Gawk* means *gape* or *stare*, *prattle* means *chatter* or *babble*, *drone* means *talk monotonously*, and *don* means *wear*.

5. **D.** "A lithe (graceful) person does not lumber (walk heavily)."

   A. A wary person does not worry . . . no, a cautious person does worry.

   B. An evasive person does not avoid . . . no, an evasive person does avoid.

   C. An egotistical person does not boast . . . no, a self-centered person probably does brag.

   (D.) A diplomatic person does not offend . . . yes, a tactful person does not offend.

   E. A tactful person does not mediate . . . no, a tactful person does bring about agreement.

6. **A.** "Subtle is the opposite of obvious."

   (A.) Vain is the opposite of modest . . . yes, egotistical is the opposite of modest.

   B. Transparent is the opposite of translucent . . . no, they are different, but not opposites.

   C. Bulbous is the opposite of bowed . . . no, they are synonyms.

   D. Wistful is the opposite of longing . . . no, they are synonyms.

   E. Elated is the opposite of euphoric . . . no, they both mean *psyched*.

7. **D.** "Friends blame Joe's *selfish* philosophy for his selfish behavior."
   Use the process of elimination. *Wistful* means *nostalgic*, *suave* means *polished* or *tactful*, and *circumspect* means *cautious*. *Solipsistic* means *self-centered* and is the best answer.

8. **C.** "Mia avoided the agents who sought to capture her; she *avoided* them by entering the tunnels of the subway."
   Eluded means *avoided*. The sentence does not indicate that she *terminated* (killed) them or that she *tousled* them (messed up their hair).

Inexplicable Frustration

Find each of the following words on the *Twilight* page number provided. Based on the way each word is used in the book, guess at its definition.

1. **Complimentary** (p. 37) might mean _____

   _____

2. **Suppress** (p. 38) might mean _____

   _____

3. **Animatedly** (p. 40) might mean _____

   _____

4. **Saturated** (p. 41) might mean _____

   _____

5. **Disheveled** (p. 43) might mean _____

   _____

6. **Scrawl** (p. 46) might mean _____

   _____

7. **Inexplicable** (p. 46) might mean _____

   _____

8. **Auburn** (p. 46) might mean _____

   _____

Let's see how you did. Check your answers, write the exact definitions, and reread the sentence in *Twilight* where each word appears. Then complete the drills.

1. **Complimentary** (p. 37) in this case means *giving compliments.* It can also mean *free,* like the complimentary sugar-free lollipops on your guidance counselor's desk.

2. **Suppress** (p. 38) means *restrain* or *prevent,* basically, **press** something down. Sometimes students see a word that they don't know and think, "I have no chance." But if you break a word apart or look for situations where you have seen the word, often you can get the gist of the meaning. Synonyms: quell, squelch.

3. **Animatedly** (p. 40) means *energetically.* This is easy to remember since animated characters in cartoons are usually more expressive and lively than real people or animals—you rarely see a depressed cartoon character; think SpongeBob. And some people think that Mr. SquarePants has no educational value!

4. **Saturated** (p. 41) means *completely soaked* or *drenched.* You've probably heard this word in Chemistry class; a solution is saturated when it cannot hold any more solvent—it's completely soaked.

5. **Disheveled** (p. 43) means *messy.* This is the second word that you've seen to describe the messiness of Edward's hair. Do you remember the first? *Tousled,* which also means *messy,* but is used especially for hair. What's with famous boys and messy hair? Edward Cullen, Harry Potter . . .

6. **Scrawl** (p. 46) means *messy writing.*

7. **Inexplicable** (p. 46) means *not explainable. In-* means *not,* and *explicable* means *explainable.* In English class, you may have been asked to write an essay that *explicates* (explains) the themes in *Romeo and Juliet.*

8. **Auburn** (p. 46) means *reddish-brown.*

Synonyms: Select the word or phrase whose meaning is closest to the word in capital letters.

Drills

1. SUPPRESS
   A. impress
   B. squall
   C. saturate
   D. compliment
   E. quell

2. INEXPLICABLE
   A. inconsequential
   B. exiled
   C. intransient
   D. mystifying
   E. lucid

3. SATURATED
   A. animated
   B. subtle
   C. full
   D. wary
   E. wistful

4. DISHEVELED
   A. tousled
   B. apprehensive
   C. statuesque
   D. inconsequential
   E. requisite

Analogies: Select the answer choice that best completes the meaning of the sentence.

5. Scrawl is to neatness as
   A. diplomacy is to tact
   B. litheness is to grace
   C. vogue is to style
   D. animation is to vitality
   E. subtlety is to heavy-handedness

6. Auburn is to color as
   A. haven is to shell
   B. burly is to build
   C. stammer is to sentence
   D. clandestine is to hatred
   E. vogue is to antagonism

Sentence Completions: Choose the word that, when inserted in the sentence, <u>best</u> fits the meaning of the sentence as a whole.

7. Despite his calming tone and air of authority, the mayor was unable to _____ the fury of the angry mob.
   A. quell
   B. compliment
   C. saturate
   D. dishevel
   E. explicate

8. The supervisor neither smiled nor frowned and hardly showed emotion at all; this _____ demeanor discomforted the employees.
   A. wistful
   B. diplomatic
   C. vain
   D. unanimated
   E. lumbering

1. **E.** *Suppress* and *quell* mean *restrain*. *Squall* on the other hand is *a sudden, powerful storm*.
2. **D.** *Inexplicable* and *mystifying* mean *not explainable*. Check out choice C, *intransient*. Do you remember this fabulous word from Group 1? *Intransience* means *not moving*. Remember that *in-* means *not*, and *trans* means *across*, so *intransient* means *not going across*, or *not budging!* And, choice E, *lucid*, means *clear*; notice *luc-*, like the Spanish word *luz* for *light*.
3. **C.** *Saturated* means *full*. Let's review the other choices. *Animated* means *lively*, *subtle* means *discreet*, *wary* means *cautious*, and *wistful* means *reminiscing* or *longing*.
4. **A.** *Disheveled* and *tousled* both mean *messy*. Tousled usually refers to hair, while disheveled can refer to anything, like your bedroom. Choice E, *requisite*, looks a lot like the word *required*, and that's exactly what it means, it's a synonym for *mandatory*.
5. **E.** "Scrawl lacks neatness."
   A . Diplomacy lacks tact . . . no, *diplomacy* means *tact*.
   B . Litheness lacks grace . . . no, *litheness* means *grace*.
   C . Vogue lacks style . . . no, *vogue* means *the latest style*.
   D . Animation lacks vitality . . . no, animation is related to *vitality* (liveliness).
   (E .) Subtlety lacks heavy-handedness . . . yes, indirectness lacks heavy-handedness.
6. **B.** "Auburn is a type of color."
   A . Haven is a type of shell . . . no, they are totally unrelated, except to maybe a clam or snail.
   (B .) Burly is a type of build . . . yes, *burly* means *a large muscular build*—think Emmett.
   C . Stammer is a type of sentence . . . no.
   D . Clandestine is a type of hatred . . . no, *clandestine* means *secretive*.
   E . Vogue is a type of antagonism . . . no, *vogue* means *style*, and *antagonism* means *hatred*.
7. **A.** "Despite his calming tone and air of authority, the mayor was unable to *calm* the fury of the angry mob."
   Quell means *calm*. *Compliment* means *praise*, *saturate* means *soak*, *dishevel* means *mess up*, and *explicate* means *explain*.
8. **D.** "The supervisor neither smiled nor frowned and hardly showed emotion at all; this *unemotional* demeanor discomforted the employees."
   Unanimated can mean *unemotional*. *Wistful* means *longing*, *diplomatic* means *tactful*, *vain* means *egotistical*, and *lumbering* means *walking awkwardly*.

Ocher Eyes

Find each of the following words on the *Twilight* page number provided. Based on the way each word is used in the book, guess at its definition.

1. **Ocher** (p. 46) might mean _____

   _____

2. **Mused** (p. 48) might mean _____

   _____

3. **Sympathetic** (p. 48) might mean _____

   _____

4. **Surmised** (p. 48) might mean _____

   _____

5. **Fathom** (p. 48) might mean _____

   _____

6. **Vitally** (p. 48) might mean _____

   _____

7. **Glum** (p. 49) might mean _____

   _____

8. **Smugly** (p. 50) might mean _____

   _____

Let's see how you did. Check your answers, write the exact definitions, and reread the sentence in *Twilight* where each word appears. Then complete the drills.

1. **Ocher** (p. 46) means *brownish-yellow colored,* like butterscotch. Someone's in a better mood after hunting . . .

2. **Mused** (p. 48) in this case means *said while reflecting (thinking).*

3. **Sympathetic** (p. 48) means *showing concern or compassion.* This is a great word to break apart. *Sym-* means *together,* and *path* refers to *feeling.* So *sympathy* (feeling together) means *showing concern.* You can use these word parts to understand a bunch of great vocab words, such as *symmetry* (measuring together) which means *having equal proportions, symbiotic* (living together) which means *a mutually beneficial relationship,* and *empathy* which means *feeling another's feelings,* or powers in the case of Peter from *Heroes!*

4. **Surmised** (p. 48) means *guessed* or *concluded.*

5. **Fathom** (p. 48) means *understand* or *comprehend.*

6. **Vitally** (p. 48) means *crucially,* like your life depends on it. In fact, the word *vital* means *full of life* or *very important.* Synonym for *vital:* imperative (very important).

7. **Glum** (p. 49) means *sad and quiet.* This is one of those words that definitely sounds like what it means. Sometimes, if I don't know a word, I ask myself, "What does it sound like? Does it sound fast or slow, lively or sad, nice or mean? Would I be complimented or insulted if a friend called me this word?" You'll be surprised how often this gives you a hint to a word's meaning. Synonyms: doleful, dour, lugubrious, melancholic, morose, sullen.

8. **Smugly** (p. 50) means *with excessive pride.* Synonyms for *smug:* arrogant, bombastic, haughty, pompous.

Synonyms: Select the word or phrase whose meaning is closest to the word in capital letters.

1. SMUG
   A. haughty
   B. vituperative
   C. superfluous
   D. surmised
   E. modest

2. SYMMETRIC
   A. ocher
   B. compendious
   C. simple
   D. even
   E. furtive

3. SYMPATHETIC
   A. aware
   B. angry
   C. compassionate
   D. musing
   E. permissive

4. FATHOM
   A. misunderstand
   B. comprehend
   C. dream
   D. suppress
   E. saturate

Analogies: Select the answer choice that best completes the meaning of the sentence.

5. Elated is to glum as
   A. thrilled is to eager
   B. vital is to haughty
   C. excited is to dour
   D. euphoric is to exiled
   E. ecstatic is to clandestine

6. Disappointment is to sullen as
   A. victory is to melancholic
   B. success is to translucent
   C. let down is to flat
   D. accomplishment is to elated
   E. stammer is to imperiled

Sentence Completions: Choose the word that, when inserted in the sentence, <u>best</u> fits the meaning of the sentence as a whole.

7. Sea anemones and clown fish have a _____ relationship, each benefiting from the presence of the other.
   A. symbiotic
   B. lugubrious
   C. haughty
   D. suppressed
   E. inexplicable

8. After witnessing the scrawl that filled his notebook, Akira was not surprised to find Diego's house equally _____.
   A. complimentary
   B. saturated
   C. bombastic
   D. disheveled
   E. dour

1. **A.** *Smug* and *haughty* both mean *conceited*. Did you recognize *vituperative* from Group 5? It is a super fancy word for *maliciously condemning* (meanly criticizing). *Superfluous* is a fun word meaning *unnecessary.* I always remember this word from a scene in *Pirates of the Caribbean: The Curse of the Black Pearl* when Johnny Depp's character is about to steal a ship and is talking to the guards at the dock. Check it out.

2. **D.** *Symmetric* means *with equal measure* or *even-looking.* The wings of a butterfly are symmetrical (evenly proportioned) to each other. Remember that *compendious* means *concise but complete,* and *furtive,* like *surreptitious,* means *secretive.*

3. **C.** *Sympathetic* means *compassionate. Musing* means *reflecting,* and *permissive* means *very lenient*—permitting too much.

4. **B.** *Fathom* and *comprehend* both mean *understand.*

5. **C.** "Elated is the opposite of glum."
   A. Thrilled is the opposite of eager . . . no, they are similar.
   B. Vital (lively) is the opposite of haughty (arrogant) . . . no.
   C. Excited is the opposite of dour (gloomy) . . . yes!
   D. Euphoric (very excited) is the opposite of exiled . . . no, they are unrelated.
   E. Ecstatic (very excited) is the opposite of clandestine (secretive) . . . no, they are unrelated.

6. **D.** "Disappointment might cause sullen feelings."
   A. Victory might cause melancholic (deeply sad) feelings . . . no.
   B. Success might cause translucent feelings . . . no, that makes no sense!
   C. A letdown might cause flat feelings . . . maybe, but not a great choice.
   D. Accomplishment might cause elated (excited) feelings . . . yes!
   E. Stammer (stutter) might cause imperiled (in danger) feelings . . . no.

7. **A.** "Sea anemones and clown fish have a *mutually beneficial* relationship, each benefiting from the presence of the other."
   Symbiotic means *mutually beneficial. Inexplicable* almost works, but there is no evidence in the sentence that says that the relationship is *unexplainable,* only that it is mutually beneficial. *Lugubrious* means *glum,* and *haughty* means *arrogant.*

8. **D.** "After witnessing the scrawl that filled his notebook, Akira was not surprised to find Diego's house equally *messy.*"
   Disheveled means *messy. Complimentary* means *praising, saturated* means *full, bombastic* means *arrogant,* and *dour* means *glum.*

Group 10
A Peripheral Peek

Find each of the following words on the *Twilight* page number provided. Based on the way each word is used in the book, guess at its definition.

1. **Despise** (p. 50) might mean _____
   _____

2. **Chivalrously** (p. 51) might mean _____
   _____

3. **Woolgathering** (p. 51) might mean _____
   _____

4. **Peripheral** (p. 52) might mean _____
   _____

5. **Veiling** (p. 53) might mean _____
   _____

6. **Reveling** in (p. 54) might mean _____
   _____

7. **Emanating** (p. 54) might mean _____
   _____

8. **Novelty** (p. 55) might mean _____
   _____

Let's see how you did. Check your answers, write the exact definitions, and reread the sentence in *Twilight* where each word appears. Then complete the drills.

1. **Despise** (p. 50) means *hate.* Synonyms: abhor, detest, disdain, loathe, scorn. You learned the word *detest* in Group 1. Okay, quick quiz. Who despises who? Name the character most despised by: a) Edward; b) Victoria; c) Jacob; d) Mike Newton; e) Rosalie. (Answers vary, talk them over with your friends . . .)

2. **Chivalrously** (p. 51) means *bravely and courteously* (especially toward women). This word is usually used to refer to knights, like in King Arthur stories. Synonym: gallant (brave).

3. **Woolgathering** (p. 51) means *daydreaming.* This word comes from a shepherd following sheep and gathering clumps of wool torn off by bushes and brambles . . . I guess shepherds daydreamed as they followed the sheep. Since we're at the farm, here are a few more great farm words:

   Arable means *good for farming* (such as arable land).
   Husbandry means *care of crops, animals, or the environment.*
   Arboreal means *relating to trees,* such as arboreal apes.
   Verdant means *green with vegetation.*

4. **Peripheral** (p. 52) means *at the edge* (rather than at the center).

5. **Veiling** (p. 53) means *covering,* like a veil is used to cover one's face. Synonym for *veil:* shroud.

6. **Reveling in** (p. 54) means *getting great enjoyment from. Revel* can also mean *engage in lively festivities,* which one would likely get great pleasure from.

7. **Emanating** (p. 54) means *radiating.*

8. **Novelty** (p. 55) means *new and unfamiliar thing.*

Synonyms: Select the word or phrase whose meaning is closest to the word in capital letters.

Drills

1. DESPISE
   A. censure
   B. veil
   C. depose
   D. muse
   E. abhor

2. GALLANT
   A. noble
   B. peripheral
   C. pale
   D. vital
   E. smug

3. EMANATE
   A. revel
   B. detest
   C. fathom
   D. sympathize
   E. radiate

4. VERDANT
   A. condemn
   B. lush
   C. denounce
   D. inconsequential
   E. lithe

Analogies: Select the answer choice that best completes the meaning of the sentence.

5. Dislike is to abhorrence as
   A. center is to periphery
   B. chivalry is to courtesy
   C. novelty is to newness
   D. fondness is to adoration
   E. arboreal is to trees

6. Husbandry is to environment as
   A. reveling is to parties
   B. woolgathering is to animals
   C. emanating is to king
   D. parenting is to children
   E. ocher is to color

Sentence Completions: Choose the word or words that, when inserted in the sentence, <u>best</u> fits the meaning of the sentence as a whole.

7. Ramirez felt great _____ for his opponent who was clearly cheating in the tennis match.
   A. disdain
   B. chivalry
   C. husbandry
   D. claustrophobia
   E. permanence

8. The farm committee declared that in order to increase the amount of _____ land, farmers must replace policies of overuse with policies of _____.
   A. verdant .. veiling
   B. arboreal .. conservation
   C. arable .. husbandry
   D. gallant .. novelty
   E. usable .. woolgathering

1. **E.** *Despise* and *abhor* mean *hate*. *Censure* almost works, but it means *officially criticize* rather than *hate*.

2. **A.** *Gallant* means *brave*. If the correct answer does not jump out, use the process of elimination:
   - A. Noble . . . maybe, *noble* means *dignified* or even *principled*.
   - B. Peripheral . . . no, *peripheral* means *the edge* of something.
   - C. Pale . . . no.
   - D. Vital . . . no, *vital* means *very important* or *lively*.
   - E. Smug . . . no, *smug* means *arrogant*.

   Okay, even if you might not have thought of *noble* meaning *gallant*, it is certainly the best choice. Sometimes standardized tests do that; they give a choice that is not perfect, but is better than the others and is therefore the correct answer.

3. **E.** *Emanate* means *radiate*.

4. **B.** *Verdant* means *green with vegetation*. Notice the similarity to the Spanish word *verde* for green! *Lush* can refer to *impressive growth of vegetation* and is the best choice. *Condemn* and *denounce* both mean *criticize,* and *lithe* means *graceful and flexible*.

5. **D.** "Dislike is less extreme than abhorrence (hatred)."
   - A. Center is less than periphery . . . no, the center is not less than the edge.
   - B. Chivalry is less than courtesy . . . no, they mean the same thing.
   - C. Novelty is less than newness . . . no, they mean the same thing.
   - D. Fondness is less than adoration . . . maybe, fondness is less extreme than adoration.
   - E. Arboreal is less than trees . . . no, *arboreal* means *pertaining to trees*.

6. **D.** "Husbandry is caring for the environment."
   - A. Reveling is caring for parties . . . no, *reveling* means *partying*.
   - B. Woolgathering is caring for animals . . . no, *woolgathering* means *daydreaming*.
   - C. Emanating is caring for the king . . . no, *emanating* means *radiating*.
   - D. Parenting is caring for children . . . yes!
   - E. Ocher is caring for color . . . no, *ocher* is a *type of color (brownish-yellow)*.

7. **A.** "Ramirez felt great <u>anger</u> for his opponent who was clearly cheating in the tennis match."

   None of the choices mean *anger*, but *disdain* means *hatred* and is the closest and therefore best choice.

8. **C.** "The farm committee declared that in order to increase the amount of <u>good</u> land, farmers must replace policies of overuse with policies of <u>not overuse/care</u>."

   Use the process of elimination, one blank at a time. Choice C is best since *arable* means *good for crops* and *husbandry* means *care of resources*.

Quiz 2

I. Let's review some of the words that you've seen in Groups 6–10. Match each of the following words to the correct definition or synonym on the right. Then check the solutions on page 171.

1. Hasty		A.	Evade
2. Opaque		B.	Suppress
3. Euphoria		C.	Rushed
4. Prevaricate		D.	Vital
5. Wary		E.	A new thing
6. Quell		F.	Not translucent
7. Auburn		G.	Reddish-brown
8. Haughty		H.	Bliss
9. Imperative		I.	Apprehensive
10. Melancholic		J.	Relating to trees
11. Loathe		K.	Bombastic
12. Gallant		L.	Morose
13. Verdant		M.	Green and lush
14. Novelty		N.	Detest
15. Arboreal		O.	Brave

II. Let's review several of the word parts that you've seen in Groups 6–10. Match each of the following word parts to the correct definition or synonym on the right. Then check the solutions on page 171.

16. Circum-		A.	Through or across
17. In-, Im-		B.	Death
18. Necro-		C.	Together
19. Path-		D.	Around
20. Trans-		E.	Feeling
21. Sym-		F.	Not

Bedlam

Find each of the following words on the *Twilight* page number provided. Based on the way each word is used in the book, guess at its definition.

1. **Providentially** (p. 56) might mean _____

   _____

2. **Bedlam** (p. 57) might mean _____

   _____

3. **Vehemently** (p. 58) might mean _____

   _____

4. **Soberly** (p. 58) might mean _____

   _____

5. **Chaotically** (p. 59) might mean _____

   _____

6. **Myriad** (p. 60) might mean _____

   _____

7. **Remorseful** (p. 61) might mean _____

   _____

8. **Ogle** (p. 61) might mean _____

   _____

Let's see how you did. Check your answers, write the exact definitions, and reread the sentence in *Twilight* where each word appears. Then complete the drills.

Definitions

1. **Providentially** (p. 56) means *fortunately* or *with divine intervention.* It comes from the word *providence,* which means *the protective care of God.* Synonyms for *providential:* auspicious, opportune.

2. **Bedlam** (p. 57) means *noise and confusion.* This word actually comes from the name of a fourteenth-century hospital for the mentally ill in London, England. Synonyms: anarchy, chaos, mayhem (remember Project Mayhem from *Fight Club*?), pandemonium, turmoil.

3. **Vehemently** (p. 58) means *with very strong feeling.* Synonyms: fervently, fervidly.

4. **Soberly** (p. 58) means *seriously and sincerely.* It also, of course, means *not drunk,* which makes sense since drunkenness is not associated with seriousness and sincerity. Synonyms for *sober:* solemn, somber.

5. **Chaotically** (p. 59) means *with complete disorder and confusion.* What word does this remind you of? Anyone? Anyone? That's right, bedlam. The word *chaotically* comes from the word *chaos,* which is a synonym for *bedlam.*

6. **Myriad** (p. 60) in this case means *many,* but it can also mean *a countless number.* Synonyms: innumerable, multifarious (many and varied), multiplicity (notice the prefix *multi-,* which means *many*), plethora (too many).

7. **Remorseful** (p. 61) means *regretful.* Synonyms: contrite, penitent, repentant.

8. **Ogle** (p. 61) means *stare with excessive, or possibly offensive, sexual desire.* This word even sounds naughty!

Synonyms: Select the word or phrase whose meaning is closest to the word in capital letters.

1. OPPORTUNE
   A. sporadic
   B. timely
   C. morose
   D. bombastic
   E. lucid

2. REMORSE
   A. condemn
   B. mayhem
   C. reveling
   D. sympathy
   E. repentance

3. ANARCHY
   A. chaos
   B. vehemence
   C. suppression
   D. scrawl
   E. evasion

4. MYRIAD
   A. numeral
   B. plethora
   C. desire
   D. turmoil
   E. night

Analogies: Select the answer choice that best completes the meaning of the sentence.

5. Fervent is to passion as
   A. chaotic is to order
   B. vehement is to novelty
   C. contrite is to regret
   D. vital is to tact
   E. circumspect is to haste

6. Sober is to solemn as
   A. innumerable is to multifarious
   B. remorseful is to proud
   C. opportune is to star-crossed
   D. sporadic is to auspicious
   E. hypersensitive is to unstipulated

Sentence Completions: Choose the word that, when inserted in the sentence, <u>best</u> fits the meaning of the sentence as a whole.

7. Marketing wiz Zach Lang is known for timing product releases perfectly; this _____ timing has earned him a stellar reputation.
   A. vehement
   B. opportune
   C. sober
   D. chaotic
   E. remorseful

8. Lijun sought a university that could accommodate his _____ interests, ranging from economics to English to yoga.
   A. chivalrous
   B. peripheral
   C. shrouded
   D. fathomed
   E. multifarious

1. **B.** *Opportune* and *timely* mean *well-timed.* Remember *sporadic* from Group 1? *Sporadic* is a synonym for *erratic* and means *irregular. Morose* means *glum, bombastic* means *arrogant,* and *lucid* means *clear.*

2. **E.** *Remorse* and *repentance* mean *regret for a wrong. Condemn* means *criticize strongly, mayhem* means *chaos, reveling* means *partying,* and *sympathy* means *compassion.* A judge might *condemn* a criminal who shows no *remorse,* but they are not synonyms.

3. **A.** *Anarchy* and *chaos* mean *absence of authority and order. Anarchy* is a great word to break apart. *A-* or *An-* means *not* or *without,* like *amoral* (not moral) and *atypical* (not typical), and *-arch* means *chief* or *rule,* like *monarchy* (rule by one) and *matriarchy* (rule by a woman—from *maternal*).

4. **B.** *Myriad* and *plethora* mean *a lot. Numeral* is a nice trick answer since it has to do with numbers, but it does not mean *a lot. Turmoil* means *chaos.*

5. **C.** "*Fervent* means a lot of passion." It's great when you can define the first word using the second.
   A . Chaotic means a lot of order . . . no, *chaotic* means *no order.*
   B . Vehement means a lot of novelty . . . no, *vehement* means *passionate.*
   C . Contrite means a lot of regret . . . yes, *contrite* means *a lot of regret.*
   D . Vital means a lot of tact . . . no, *vital* means *energetic.*
   E . Circumspect means a lot of haste . . . no, *circumspect* means *cautious.*

6. **A.** "*Sober* is a synonym for *solemn.*" Lots of "s" words here.
   A . Innumerable is a synonym for multifarious . . . yes, both words mean *many.*
   B . Remorseful is a synonym for proud . . . no.
   C . Opportune (well-timed) is a synonym for star-crossed (unlucky) . . . no, they're unrelated.
   D . Sporadic (erratic) is a synonym for auspicious (fortunate) . . . no, they are unrelated.
   E . Hypersensitive is a synonym for unstipulated . . . no, *hypersensitive* means *very sensitive* (*hyper-* means *very*), and *unstipulated* means *not required.*

7. **B.** "Marketing wiz Zach Lang is known for timing product releases perfectly; this _perfect_ timing has earned him a stellar reputation."
   Opportune means *well-timed.*

8. **E.** "Lijun sought a university that could accommodate his _many_ interests, ranging from economics to English to yoga."
   Multifarious means *many and varied.* The word "range" in the question tells you that you need a word to express this array of interests.

Group 12
Livid Angel

Find each of the following words on the *Twilight* page number provided. Based on the way each word is used in the book, guess at its definition.

1. **Patronizing** (p. 62) might mean _____

   _____

2. **Flourish** (p. 63) might mean _____

   _____

3. **Amended** (p. 63) might mean _____

   _____

4. **Derision** (p. 65) might mean _____

   _____

5. **Flitted** (p. 65) might mean _____

   _____

6. **Livid** (p. 65) might mean _____

   _____

7. **Frigidly** (p. 65) might mean _____

   _____

8. **Sullenly** (p. 66) might mean _____

   _____

Let's see how you did. Check your answers, write the exact definitions, and reread the sentence in *Twilight* where each word appears. Then complete the drills.

Definitions

1. **Patronizing** (p. 62) in this case means *kind but with a superior attitude.* It also means *supporting* or *being a customer,* like shopping at a store or eating at a restaurant. Standardized tests love to use words with multiple meanings. On a reading comprehension question, make sure to check the word in the passage to see which meaning is appropriate. Synonyms: condescending, demeaning, denigrating.

2. **Flourish** (p. 63) in this case means *an exaggerated gesture* or even *a decorative curve in handwriting*—like the kind you might see from someone much older-looking than Carlisle . . . *Flourish* can also mean *to thrive.*

3. **Amended** (p. 63) means *added to correct or improve*—the addition of the Bill of Rights and other *amendments* improved the United States Constitution.

4. **Derision** (p. 65) means *harsh mockery.* Synonyms: disparagement, ridicule, scorn.

5. **Flitted** (p. 65) means *moved quickly.*

6. **Livid** (p. 65) means *really, really mad.* Synonyms: incensed, infuriated, irate.

7. **Frigidly** (p. 65) means *coldly,* since *frigid* means *cold.* It also implies *not friendly,* like giving someone "the cold shoulder." Synonyms: callously (coldly, but also cruelly), frostily, impersonally.

8. **Sullenly** (p. 66) means *with a gloomy and irritable mood. Sullen* was a synonym for *glum* in Group 9. *Glum* means *sad and **quiet*** whereas *sullen* means *sad and **irritable.*** Synonyms for *sullen:* doleful, dour, glum, lugubrious, melancholic, morose, surly.

Synonyms: Select the word or phrase whose meaning is closest to the word in capital letters.

1. FLOURISH
   - A. eaves
   - B. bedlam
   - C. extravagant display
   - D. veiled distaste
   - E. scrawled note

2. IRATE
   - A. jolly
   - B. frigid
   - C. livid
   - D. sullen
   - E. sober

3. AMEND
   - A. compliment
   - B. modify
   - C. patronize
   - D. deride
   - E. flit

4. SCORN
   - A. remorse
   - B. revel
   - C. surmise
   - D. quell
   - E. deride

Analogies: Select the answer choice that best completes the meaning of the sentence.

5. Flourish is to ornamental as
   - A. sullen is to added
   - B. flitted is to slow
   - C. disparage is to complimented
   - D. scrawl is to muddled
   - E. incensed is to euphoric

6. Sullen is to elated as
   - A. prevaricating is to evading
   - B. ogling is to gawking
   - C. condescending is to admiring
   - D. shrouding is to covering
   - E. remorseful is to regretful

Sentence Completions: Choose the word or words that, when inserted in the sentence, <u>best</u> fits the meaning of the sentence as a whole.

7. Jennifer resented the teacher's _____ tone: it was not quite _____ or mocking, but did not seem sincere in its kindness.
   - A. amended .. livid
   - B. doleful .. morose
   - C. patronizing .. disparaging
   - D. demeaning .. glum
   - E. compelling .. frigid

8. A fan of ornate lettering, Trevis always ended his handwritten notes with a terminal _____.
   - A. flourish
   - B. amendment
   - C. vehemence
   - D. remorse
   - E. novelty

1. **C.** *Flourish* means *an extravagant display. Eaves* means the *overhang of a roof, bedlam* is *chaos, veiled distaste* means *indirectly expressed distaste,* and *scrawl* means *messy handwriting.*

2. **C.** *Irate* and *livid* mean *very mad. Frigid* means *cold* or *unfriendly, sullen* means *sad and irritable,* and *sober* means *serious.*

3. **B.** *Amend* and *modify* both mean *alter. Compliment* means *praise, patronize* means *show kindness tinged with superiority, deride* means *ridicule,* and *flit* means *move quickly.*

4. **E.** *Scorn* and *deride* both mean *ridicule.* Use the process of elimination—cross off answers that you are sure don't work and choose the best of what's left. *Remorse* means *regret, revel* means *party, surmise* means *guess,* and *quell* means *suppress.*

5. **D.** "Flourish is an ornamental gesture."
   A. Sullen is an added gesture . . . no, *sullen* means *sad and irritable.*
   B. Flitted is a slow gesture . . . no, *flitted* means *moved quickly.*
   C. Disparage is a complimented gesture . . . no, disparage is the opposite of compliment.
   (D.) Scrawl is a muddled gesture . . . yes, *scrawl* is *muddled (messy) handwriting.*
   E. Incensed is a euphoric gesture . . . no, *incensed* is *angry* and *euphoric* is *psyched.*

6. **C.** "Sullen is the opposite of elated."
   A. Prevaricating is the opposite of evading . . . no, they mean the same thing.
   B. Ogling is the opposite of gawking . . . no, they are different kinds of looks, but not opposites.
   (C.) Condescending is the opposite of admiring . . . maybe, they are close to being opposites.
   D. Shrouding (covering) is the opposite of covering . . . no.
   E. Remorseful (regretful) is the opposite of regretful . . . no.

7. **C.** "Jennifer resented the teacher's *insincerely kind* tone: it was not quite *mocking* or mocking, but did not seem sincere in its kindness."
   Use the process of elimination, one blank at a time. Choice C is best, since *patronizing* means *kind but with superiority,* and *disparaging* means *mocking.*

8. **A.** "A fan of ornate lettering, Trevis always ended his handwritten notes with a terminal *ornateness.*"
   The phrase "A fan of ornate lettering" tells you how he would end his notes and tells you what you need for the blank. *Flourish* means *ornate lettering.* A person might end a letter with an amendment, vehemence, remorse, or a novelty, but none of these are supported by evidence in the sentence.

Chagrin

Find each of the following words on the *Twilight* page number provided. Based on the way each word is used in the book, guess at its definition.

1. **Converge** (p. 66) might mean _____

_____

2. **Hysterics** (p. 66) might mean _____

_____

3. **Chagrin** (p. 69) might mean _____

_____

4. **Tenor** (p. 70) might mean _____

_____

5. **Broach** (p. 72) might mean _____

_____

6. **Floundered** (p. 72) might mean _____

_____

7. **Reflexively** (p. 72) might mean _____

_____

8. **Dejected** (p. 73) might mean _____

_____

Let's see how you did. Check your answers, write the exact definitions, and reread the sentence in *Twilight* where each word appears. Then complete the drills.

Definitions

1. **Converge** (p.66) means *approach and join together.* Like *com-* from Group 2, *con-* means *together* (just as *con* means *with* in Spanish).

2. **Hysterics** (p. 66) in this case means *a very emotional reaction.* It can also mean *uncontrollable laughter.* You can see how the two definitions are related, like crying from laughing so hard. There is another great vocab word that is related to this word: *histrionic,* which means *very dramatic* or *pertaining to the theater.* I've seen this word stump tons of kids on the SAT, but it won't stump you now that you've seen its connection to the word *hysterics.*

3. **Chagrin** (p. 69) means *embarrassment.* Synonym: mortification (I was mortified!). Have you ever been so embarrassed that you said, "I almost died!" Well, *mort-* means *death,* and that's exactly where the word *mortified* comes from!

4. **Tenor** (p. 70) in this case means *tone. Tenor* can also mean *a singing voice between baritone and alto.* Again, you can see where this meaning comes from—notice the connection between *tone* and *singing.*

5. **Broach** (p. 72) means *approach* or *raise for discussion,* not to be confused with *brooch,* the large multicolored butterfly pin that your great aunt wears on her lavender suit jacket.

6. **Floundered** (p. 72) means *struggled uncomfortably,* like a flounder fish flopping and struggling in very shallow water or mud.

7. **Reflexively** (p. 72) means *unconsciously* or *automatically,* like a reflex action.

8. **Dejected** (p. 73) means *made sad.* This is an interesting word to break apart. *De-* means *down,* as in *descend* (climb down) or *depressed* (pressed down—sad). And *–ject* refers to *throw,* like *eject* (throw out), so *dejected* refers to *thrown down*—made sad.

Synonyms: Select the word or phrase whose meaning is closest to the word in capital letters.

1. CHAGRIN
   A. floundering
   B. converging
   C. embarrassment
   D. rejection
   E. tenor

2. FLOUNDER
   A. converge
   B. swim
   C. flourish
   D. patronize
   E. struggle

3. HISTRIONIC
   A. theatrical
   B. reflexive
   C. erratic
   D. genuine
   E. opportune

4. BROACH
   A. deject
   B. approach
   C. flit
   D. deride
   E. converge

Analogies: Select the answer choice that best completes the meaning of the sentence.

5. Broach is to evade as
   A. chagrin is to mortify
   B. reflexive is to planned
   C. flounder is to struggle
   D. deject is to reject
   E. amend is to change

6. Sullen is to tenor as
   A. derision is to ridicule
   B. livid is to appreciation
   C. frigid is to appliance
   D. ogle is to look
   E. anarchy is to democracy

Sentence Completions: Choose the word or words that, when inserted in the sentence, best fits the meaning of the sentence as a whole.

7. Scott knew that if he did not call Leigh immediately, he might _____ and never _____ the topic of asking her to the movies.
   A. flounder .. broach
   B. emanate .. engage
   C. flourish .. flitter
   D. patronize .. deride
   E. converge .. raise

8. From the attitude and _____ of the lecturer's remarks, Devash deduced that he was an environmental advocate.
   A. chagrin
   B. tenor
   C. dejection
   D. sobriety
   E. empathy

1. **C.** *Chagrin* means *embarrassment.* Choice D, *rejection,* might cause embarrassment, but is not a synonym. *Floundering* means *struggling, converging* means *coming together,* and *tenor* means *tone.*

2. **E.** *Flounder* means *struggle.* Watch out for a choice like *swim,* which relates to a fish, but is not the meaning of this word. *Flourish* means *extravagant gesture,* and *patronize* means *speak kindly but with superiority.*

3. **A.** *Histrionic* means *dramatic* or *theatrical. Reflexive* means *automatic, erratic* means *unpredictable, genuine* means *real,* and *opportune* means *well-timed* or *lucky.*

4. **B.** *Broach* means *bring up in conversation.* Cross off answers that you are **sure** don't work, and then choose the best of what is left. Choices A, C, and D are way out. Choice E, *converge,* does not work as well as Choice B, *approach.* Remember, if you need more than a few steps to relate the word, then it's not the correct answer.

5. **B.** "Broach (bring up) is the opposite of evade (avoid)."
   - A. Chagrin is the opposite of mortify . . . no, they both mean *embarrass.*
   - Ⓑ Reflexive is the opposite of planned . . . yes, *reflexive* means *automatic* or *unplanned.*
   - C. Flounder is the opposite of struggle . . . no, *flounder* means *struggle.*
   - D. Deject is the opposite of reject . . . no, *deject* means *make sad,* and *reject* means *refuse.*
   - E. Amend is the opposite of change . . . no, *amend* means *change.*

6. **D.** "Sullen is a type of tenor (mood)."
   - A. Derision is a type of ridicule . . . not really, *derision* is *ridicule.*
   - B. Livid is a type of appreciation . . . no, *livid* means *furious.*
   - C. Frigid is a type of appliance . . . no, but funny; *frigid* means *cold,* and Frigidaire is a brand of refrigerator!
   - Ⓓ Ogle is a type of look . . . yes, *ogle* is a *potentially offensive look.*
   - E. Anarchy is a type of democracy . . . no, *anarchy* and *democracy* are *types of government.*

7. **A.** "Scott knew that if he did not call Leigh immediately, he might *never ask* and never *bring up* the topic of asking her to the movies."
   Choice A works best. *Flounder* means *stumble,* and *broach* means *bring up.*

8. **B.** "From the attitude and *attitude* of the lecturer's remarks, Devash deduced that he was an environmental advocate."
   Tenor means *tone* or *attitude.* The speaker *might* have shown *sobriety* (seriousness) or *empathy* (understanding), but these are not supported by evidence in the sentence.

Muted Purgatory?

Find each of the following words on the *Twilight* page number provided. Based on the way each word is used in the book, guess at its definition.

1. **Pathetic** (p. 74) might mean _____

   _____

2. **Petulance** (p. 74) might mean _____

   _____

3. **Coherently** (p. 74) might mean _____

   _____

4. **Jubilant** (p. 78) might mean _____

   _____

5. **Purgatory** (p. 79) might mean _____

   _____

6. **Muted** (p. 81) might mean _____

   _____

7. **Wheeling** (p. 83) might mean _____

   _____

8. **Enunciated** (p. 83) might mean _____

   _____

Let's see how you did. Check your answers, write the exact definitions, and reread the sentence in *Twilight* where each word appears. Then complete the drills.

Definitions

1. **Pathetic** (p.74) means *pitiful*. You already know that *path-* refers to *feeling; pathetic* refers to *something that arouses **feelings** of pity.*

2. **Petulance** (p. 74) means *sulky bad-temperedness.* Petulance even sounds unpleasant. Doesn't your face contort as you say it? Synonym: peevishness (so easy to remember when you think of the grumpy and mischievous poltergeist, Peeves, in the *Harry Potter* series!).

3. **Coherently** (p. 74) means *in a clear, logical, and consistent way.* When Bella looks at Edward, she has difficulty thinking clearly and coherently. You already have a great synonym for *coherent* from the solutions in Group 8: lucid.

4. **Jubilant** (p. 78) means *very happy or even triumphant.* You have a great word for this already, too. Do you remember it? From Group 6, you have *elated* and its synonyms: ecstatic, euphoric, and rapturous. Okay, quick quiz: What made Jessica elated on page 30 of *Twilight?*

5. **Purgatory** (p. 79) means *a place of misery.*

6. **Muted** (p. 81) means *quiet* or *softened.* That's why the "mute" button turns off the volume on your phone, TV, or computer. Synonym: subdued (like subtle).

7. **Wheeling** (p. 83) in this case means *turning quickly.* It can, of course, also mean *moving something in a vehicle that has wheels.* This is a perfect example of a word with several meanings that the SAT, ACT, GED, or SSAT might use in a reading comprehension question. To determine the meaning of a word, read the words and sentences around it. This is also useful on the ACT and GED Science sections—they never test whether you've memorized science terms; they always define terms in the passage!

8. **Enunciated** (p. 83) sounds like "announced" and means *pronounced clearly.*

Synonyms: Select the word or phrase whose meaning is closest to the word in capital letters.

1. PATHETIC
   A. shared
   B. hysterical
   C. subdued
   D. lucid
   E. pitiful

2. JUBILANT
   A. elated
   B. mortified
   C. floundering
   D. livid
   E. demeaned

3. MUTED
   A. subdued
   B. wheeling
   C. chary
   D. euphoric
   E. coherent

4. PETULANT
   A. circumspect
   B. coherent
   C. sullen
   D. frigid
   E. vehement

Analogies: Select the answer choice that best completes the meaning of the sentence.

5. Jubilant is to dejected as
   A. wary is to hasty
   B. coherent is to elucidated
   C. evasive is to lumbering
   D. purgatory is to bedlam
   E. noble is to verbose

6. Petulant is to callous as
   A. chuckling is to hysterics
   B. flitting is to ogling
   C. necrophobic is to death
   D. apprehensive is to lithe
   E. mandatory is to
      compulsory

Sentence Completions: Choose the word that, when inserted in the sentence, <u>best</u> fits the meaning of the sentence as a whole.

7. The inhabitants of the remote village were _____ in their dealings with outsiders; the few strangers that they had met had earned this mistrust.
   A. circumspect
   B. petulant
   C. jubilant
   D. muted
   E. enunciated

8. The singer was known for her sulky outbursts whenever she did not get her way; because they enjoyed her music, the public tolerated this _____ behavior.
   A. pallid
   B. petulant
   C. enunciated
   D. reflexive
   E. mortified

1. **E.** *Pathetic* means *pitiful.* *Hysterical* means *very emotional* or *very funny.*

2. **A.** *Jubilant* and *elated* both mean *psyched.* *Mortified* means *embarrassed, floundering* means *struggling,* *livid* means *very angry,* and *demeaned* means *disrespected.*

3. **A.** *Muted* means *quiet* or *subdued.* *Wheeling* means *turning, chary* means *cautious, euphoric* means *very happy,* and *coherent* means *clear.*

4. **C.** *Petulant* and *sullen* mean *irritable.* *Circumspect* means *cautious, frigid* means *cold,* and *vehement* means *passionate.*

5. **A.** "Jubilant (happy and triumphant) is the opposite of dejected (sad and defeated)."

    Great review! Look at all these great words that you now know:

    (A.) Wary is the opposite of hasty . . . yes, cautious can be the opposite of rushed.

    B . Coherent is the opposite of elucidated . . . no, clear is not the opposite of clarified.

    C . Evasive is the opposite of lumbering . . . no, avoiding is not the opposite of moving slowly and awkwardly.

    D. Purgatory is the opposite of bedlam . . . no, the words are different, but not opposites. *Purgatory* is *a place of suffering,* and *bedlam* is *a chaotic place.*

    E . Noble is the opposite of verbose . . . no, dignified is not the opposite of wordy.

6. **A.** "Petulant (grumpy) is less extreme than callous (grumpy and cruel)."

    (A.) Chuckling is less extreme than hysterics . . . yes, chuckling is less extreme than uncontrollable laughter.

    B . Flitting is less extreme than ogling . . . no.

    C . Necrophobic is less extreme than death . . . no, *necrophobic* is *having a fear of death.*

    D. Apprehensive is less extreme than lithe . . . no.

    E . Mandatory is less extreme than compulsory . . . no.

7. **A.** "The inhabitants of the remote village were _mistrustful_ in their dealings with outsiders; the few strangers that they had met had earned this mistrust."

    Circumspect means *cautious.* They may have been *petulant* (grumpy), *jubilant* (psyched), or *muted* (quiet), but you only have evidence in the sentence for *cautious.*

8. **B.** "The singer was known for her sulky outbursts whenever she did not get her way; because they enjoyed her music, the public tolerated this _sulky outbursting_ behavior."

    Petulant means *bad-tempered.* Be careful of a choice like *enunciated,* which is related to singing, but does not work to fill the blank. That's why you think of a word you want before you look at the choices.

Prudent Friendship?

Find each of the following words on the *Twilight* page number provided. Based on the way each word is used in the book, guess at its definition.

1. **Finite** (p. 83) might mean _____

_____

2. **Prudent** (p. 84) might mean _____

_____

3. **Disparaging** (p. 85) might mean _____

_____

4. **Unerringly** (p. 86) might mean _____

_____

5. **Abstraction** (p. 86) might mean _____

_____

6. **Wryly** (p. 88) might mean _____

_____

7. **Dubious** (p. 88) might mean _____

_____

8. **Befuddled** (p. 89) might mean _____

_____

60 Let's see how you did. Check your answers, write the exact definitions, and reread the sentence in *Twilight* where each word appears. Then complete the drills.

Definitions

1. **Finite** (p. 83) means *limited,* basically finishable.

2. **Prudent** (p. 84) means *sensible* or *acting with regard for the future.* If you've ever seen *Saturday Night Live* reruns of Dana Carvey impersonating George H. W. Bush, then you've heard him say "prudent." Former President Bush was famous for using that word a lot. The SAT and ACT love to use an antonym for *prudent: myopic*—it means *shortsighted, not thinking about the future.*

3. **Disparaging** (p. 85) means *disapproving.* This is a great word to break apart. *Dis-* means *not, par* means *equal,* and *-age* can denote *the product of an action.* Perfect! So *disparaging* is *the product of acting like someone is not your equal,* i.e. disapproving! You saw this word as a synonym for *derision* in Group 12. Synonyms: censorious, reproachful.

4. **Unerringly** (p. 86) in this case implies *always.* It also means *always right.* That's easy to remember, since basically, *unerringly* means *without making an error.*

5. **Abstraction** (p. 86) means *thoughts* or *preoccupation.* Synonym: pensiveness.

6. **Wryly** (p. 88) means *with dry humor.* That's easy to remember since *wry* rhymes with *dry.*

7. **Dubious** (p. 88) means *doubtful* or *hesitant.*

8. **Befuddled** (p. 89) means *unable to think clearly.* Bella tends to get that way around Edward. Synonyms: addled, muddled. *Befuddled* is the opposite of *coherent.*

1. FINITE
   A. vigilant
   B. chary
   C. jubilant
   D. limited
   E. muted

2. PRUDENT
   A. enunciated
   B. sensible
   C. dejected
   D. omnipresent
   E. amended

3. ABSTRACT
   A. myopic
   B. wary
   C. theoretical
   D. unerring
   E. literal

4. DUBIOUS
   A. hesitant
   B. incensed
   C. sullen
   D. vehement
   E. abhorrent

Analogies: Select the answer choice that best completes the meaning of the sentence.

5. Disparage is to revere as
   A. finite is to limited
   B. prudent is to unwise
   C. dubious is to doubtful
   D. addled is to muddled
   E. wry is to dry

6. Befuddled is to coherent as
   A. myopic is to short-sighted
   B. pensive is to thoughtful
   C. bulbous is to flat
   D. petulant is to sulky
   E. hesitant is to dubious

Sentence Completions: Choose the word that, when inserted in the sentence, <u>best</u> fits the meaning of the sentence as a whole.

7. The environmental commission advised that unconstrained use of finite resources was not _____ and would certainly lead to shortages.
   A. disparaging
   B. dubious
   C. prudent
   D. abstract
   E. compelling

8. The teacher complimented Matty's paper on its _____ presentation, with lucid organization and clear explanation of all themes.
   A. muted
   B. enunciated
   C. compendious
   D. coherent
   E. converging

1. **D.** *Finite* means *limited*. *Vigilant* means *watchful*, *chary* means *cautious*, *jubilant* means *happy*, and *muted* means *subdued*.

2. **B.** *Prudent* means *sensible*, like to not hang out with a vampire. *Enunciated* means *pronounced clearly*, *dejected* means *made sad*, *omnipresent* means *widespread*, and *amended* means *changed*.

3. **C.** *Abstract* means *pertaining to thoughts or ideas*. That's exactly what *theoretical* means. *Myopic* is a great word meaning *shortsighted*, *wary* means *cautious*, *unerring* means *correct*, and *literal* means *actual*.

4. **A.** *Dubious* means *doubtful* or *hesitant*. If you're not sure, use the process of elimination—cross off answers that you are **sure** don't work and choose the best of what's left. *Incensed* means *angry*, *sullen* means *grumpy*, *vehement* means *passionate*, and *abhorrent* means *hateful* (from the word *abhor*).

5. **B.** "Disparage (look down on) is the opposite of revere (strongly admire)."
   - A. Finite is the opposite of limited . . . no, they mean the same thing.
   - (B.) Prudent is the opposite of unwise . . . yes, *prudent* means *sensible* or *wise*.
   - C. Dubious is the opposite of doubtful . . . no, they mean the same thing.
   - D. Addled is the opposite of muddled . . . no, they mean the same thing.
   - E. Wry is the opposite of dry . . . no, *wry* means *with dry humor.*

6. **C.** "Befuddled (confused) is the opposite of coherent (clear-headed)."
   - A. Myopic is the opposite of shortsighted . . . no, they have the same meaning.
   - B. Pensive is the opposite of thoughtful . . . no, they have the same meaning.
   - (C.) Bulbous is the opposite of flat . . . yes.
   - D. Petulant is the opposite of sulky . . . no, they both mean *irritable* or *in a bad mood.*
   - E. Hesitant is the opposite of dubious . . . no, they have the same meaning.

7. **C.** "The environmental commission advised that unconstrained use of finite resources was not *advisable* and would certainly lead to shortages." *Prudent* means *sensible*. Choice E, *compelling*, means *convincing* and almost works, but the committee is not saying that unconstrained use is *unconvincing*—they are *warning* against it.

8. **D.** "The teacher complimented Matty's paper on its *lucid/clear* presentation, with lucid organization and clear explanation of all themes." *Coherent* means *clear and organized*. *Muted* means *subdued*, *enunciated* means *spoken clearly*, *compendious* means *concise but complete*, and *converging* means *meeting*.

Quiz 3

I. Let's review some of the words that you've seen in Groups 11–15. Match each of the following words to the correct definition or synonym on the right. Then check the solutions on page 171.

1. Vehement	A. Chaos
2. Myriad	B. Theatrical
3. Anarchy	C. Passionate
4. Livid	D. Plethora
5. Morose	E. Embarrass
6. Chagrin	F. Irate
7. Tenor	G. Circumspect
8. Histrionic	H. Irritable
9. Wary	I. Articulate
10. Petulant	J. Sullen
11. Muted	K. Tone
12. Enunciate	L. Subdued
13. Prudent	M. Shortsighted
14. Myopic	N. Doubtful
15. Dubious	O. Wise

II. Let's review several of the word parts that you've seen in Groups 11–15. Match each of the following word parts to the correct definition or synonym on the right. Then check the solutions on page 171.

16. Multi-	A. Not
17. Hyper-	B. With or together
18. Com-, Con-	C. Many
19. Mort-	D. Death
20. Dis-	E. Equal
21. Par-	F. Over or very

Impenetrable Eyes

Find each of the following words on the *Twilight* page number provided. Based on the way each word is used in the book, guess at its definition.

1. **Offhand** (p. 89) might mean _____

   _____

2. **Vacillating** (p. 89) might mean _____

   _____

3. **Cryptic** (p. 90) might mean _____

   _____

4. **Pariah** (p. 90) might mean _____

   _____

5. **Qualify** (p. 91) might mean _____

   _____

6. **Miffed** (p. 92) might mean _____

   _____

7. **Impenetrable** (p. 92) might mean _____

   _____

8. **Inaudible** (p. 93) might mean _____

   _____

BORDERS®

BORDERS
BOOKS AND MUSIC
162 E. MAIN STREET
MT. KISCO, NY 10549
914-241-8387

SALE
STORE: 0219   REG: 03/34   TRAN#: 2348
08/21/2009   EMP: 10738

I AM MESSENGER
8357039   JO T   8.95

Subtotal   8.95

BR: 8441221416

Subtotal   8.95
NY 7.375%   .66
1 Item   Total   9.61
CASH   10.00
Cash Change Due   .39

08/21/2009 08:04PM

BORDERS.

Returns

Returns of merchandise purchased from a Borders,
Borders Express or Waldenbooks retail store will be

permitted only if presented in saleable condition accompanied by the original sales receipt or Borders gift receipt within the time periods specified below. Returns accompanied by the original sales receipt must be made within 30 days of purchase and the purchase price will be refunded in the same form as the original purchase. Returns accompanied by the original Borders gift receipt must be made within 60 days of purchase and the purchase price will be refunded in the form of a return gift card.

Exchanges of opened audio books, music, videos, video games, software and electronics will be permitted subject to the same time periods and receipt requirements as above and can be made for the same item only.

Periodicals, newspapers, comic books, food and drink, digital downloads, gift cards, return gift cards, items marked "non-returnable," "final sale" or the like and out-of-print, collectible or pre-owned items cannot be returned or exchanged.

Returns and exchanges to a Borders, Borders Express or Waldenbooks retail store of merchandise purchased from Borders.com may be permitted in certain circumstances. See Borders.com for details.

BORDERS.

Returns

Returns of merchandise purchased from a Borders, Borders Express or Waldenbooks retail store will be permitted only if presented in saleable condition accompanied by the original sales receipt or Borders gift receipt within the time periods specified below. Returns accompanied by the original sales receipt must be made within 30 days of purchase and the purchase price will be refunded in the same form as the original purchase. Returns accompanied by the original Borders gift receipt must be made within 60 days of purchase and the purchase price will be refunded in the form of a return gift card.

Exchanges of opened audio books, music, videos, video games, software and electronics will be permitted subject to the same time periods and receipt requirements as above and can be made for the same item only.

Periodicals, newspapers, comic books, food and drink, digital downloads, gift cards, return gift cards, items

and reread the sentence in *Twilight* where each word appears. Then
complete the drills.

1. **Offhand** (p. 89) means *casual and possibly rude,* like making a
   quick, slightly mean jab at a friend when you're in a bad mood.
   Synonyms: brusque, cavalier, flippant, tactless.

2. **Vacillating** (p. 89) means *wavering between two decisions.* This
   reminds me of the *oscillate* option on a fan, which makes it move
   back and forth. It also reminds me of the *cilia* of a paramecium
   that you see swaying under the microscope in science class.

3. **Cryptic** (p. 90) means *mysterious.* This word relates to the word
   crypt—a hidden tomb. You can see the connection. There are
   tons of great synonyms for *cryptic:* abstruse, ambiguous, arcane,
   enigmatic, oracular, recondite.

4. **Pariah** (p. 90) means *outcast.* Not to be confused with hip-hop duo
   OutKast, who did in fact come up with their name when looking
   for a synonym for *misfit.*

5. **Qualify** (p. 91) in this case means *give reservations* or *make less
   complete.* (Of course, it can also mean *gain eligibility,* like *qualify*
   for the semifinals.) The SAT, ACT, and SSAT love this word!
   Standardized tests tend to choose reading comprehension
   passages with mild, rather than extreme, emotions. As a result,
   they often use words like *qualify* in the answer choices. If a
   question asks how the author of a passage feels about a character
   in the passage, the answer might be "qualified admiration," instead
   of "total admiration." Qualified admiration is less extreme, and
   more subtle or muted. Synonym for *qualified:* tempered.

6. **Miffed** (p. 92) means *annoyed.* Synonyms: irked, peeved (like
   Peeves the poltergeist).

7. **Impenetrable** (p. 92) means *impossible to enter or understand.* That's
   easy to remember since *impenetrable* basically means *not penetrable.*
   In fact, like *a-, an-,* and *in-; im-* also means *not,* as in **im**possible (not
   possible) and **im**probable (not probable).

8. **Inaudible** (p. 93) means *not hearable.*

Synonyms: Select the word or phrase whose meaning is closest to the word in capital letters.

1. VACILLATE
   A. waver
   B. irk
   C. err
   D. mute
   E. enunciate

2. PARIAH
   A. community
   B. niche
   C. eaves
   D. antagonist
   E. outcast

3. CRYPTIC
   A. miffed
   B. impenetrable
   C. enigmatic
   D. inaudible
   E. ocher

4. OFFHAND
   A. casual
   B. surreptitious
   C. clandestine
   D. lissome
   E. supple

Analogies: Select the answer choice that best completes the meaning of the sentence.

5. Qualify is to lessen as
   A. supplement is to add
   B. vacillate is to steady
   C. irk is to please
   D. disparage is to flatter
   E. befuddle is to enlighten

6. Pariah is to exile as
   A. diplomat is to purgatory
   B. niche is to haven
   C. claustrophobic is to bedlam
   D. corpse is to crypt
   E. vampire is to Phoenix

Sentence Completions: Choose the word that, when inserted in the sentence, best fits the meaning of the sentence as a whole.

7. Mr. Manfredi let Anita know that he did not appreciate her offhand remark and that such _____ behavior would not be tolerated.
   A. cryptic
   B. inaudible
   C. flippant
   D. vacillating
   E. tempered

8. The professor _____ so often on his opinion regarding the Big Bang theory that his colleagues considered him inconsistent.
   A. vacillated
   B. qualified
   C. erred
   D. reveled
   E. mused

1. **A.** *Vacillate* means *alternate*. That's also what *waver* can mean, like to wave your hand back and forth.
2. **E.** *Pariah* means *outcast*. A *niche* is *an appropriate situation*, and *eaves* is *the overhang of a roof past the wall of a house*.
3. **C.** *Cryptic* and *enigmatic* mean *mysterious*. *Miffed* means *angry*, *impenetrable* means *impossible to understand*, *inaudible* means *impossible to hear*, and *ocher* means *brownish-yellow*.
4. **A.** *Offhand* means *casual*. *Surreptitious* and *clandestine* are fabulous words for *secretive*, and *lissome* and *supple* are terrific words for *graceful*.
5. **A.** "Qualify is to lessen something."
   - (A.) Supplement is to add something . . . yes.
   - B . Vacillate is to steady something . . . no, the opposite.
   - C . Irk is to please something . . . no, *irk* means *to make angry*.
   - D. Disparage is to flatter something . . . no, the opposite.
   - E . Befuddle (confuse) is to enlighten (clarify) something . . . no, the opposite.
6. **D.** "A pariah (outcast) might live in exile."
   - A . A diplomat (ambassador) might live in purgatory . . . maybe, but there is no relationship, it makes no sense.
   - B . A niche might live in a haven (place of safety) . . . no, they are unrelated.
   - C . A claustrophobic (person afraid of small spaces) might live in bedlam (chaos) . . . maybe, but the words are totally unrelated.
   - (D.) A corpse might live (so to speak) in a crypt . . . sure, that works.
   - E . A vampire might live in Phoenix . . . no way, too sunny!
7. **C.** "Mr. Manfredi let Anita know that he did not appreciate her offhand remark and that such *offhand* behavior would not be tolerated."
   Flippant and *offhand* mean *casual and possibly offensive*.
8. **A.** "The professor *was inconsistent* so often on his opinion regarding the Big Bang theory that his colleagues considered him inconsistent."
   Vacillated means *wavered* or *was inconsistent*. Choice C, *erred*, might seem like it could work, but the sentence does not indicate that he made an error, only that he wavered.

Ominous Blood

Find each of the following words on the *Twilight* page number provided. Based on the way each word is used in the book, guess at its definition.

1. **Ominous** (p. 94) might mean _____

_____

2. **Sterile** (p. 94) might mean _____

_____

3. **Micro-** (p. 94) might mean _____

_____

4. **Lancet** (p. 94) might mean _____

_____

5. **Convulsively** (p. 95) might mean _____

_____

6. **Sagely** (p. 98) might mean _____

_____

7. **Loathes** (p. 99) might mean _____

_____

8. **Infinitesimally** (p. 103) might mean _____

_____

Let's see how you did. Check your answers, write the exact definitions, and reread the sentence in *Twilight* where each word appears. Then complete the drills.

1. **Ominous** (p. 94) means *threatening,* like seeing a bad omen. Synonyms: foreboding, inauspicious (opposite of auspicious and opportune), menacing.

2. **Sterile** (p. 94) in this case means *totally clean, free of bacteria.* It can also mean *uninspiring, unproductive,* or *unable to produce offspring.*

3. **Micro-** (p. 94) means *small.* Let's look at two *micro-* words:

   Microscope: micro- means *small,* and *-scope* means *an instrument for observing,* so *microscope* is *an instrument for <u>observing</u> very <u>small</u> objects.*

   Microphone: -phone means *an instrument that works with sound,* so *microphone* is *an instrument that makes small sounds larger.*

4. **Lancet** (p. 94) in this case means *a small surgical knife with a sharp point.*

5. **Convulsively** (p. 95) means *with a sudden, involuntary movement.*

6. **Sagely** (p. 98) means *wisely,* like a *sage* (wise person). Synonyms for *wise:* astute (using wisdom for one's own benefit), sagacious, shrewd.

7. **Loathes** (p. 99) means *hates.* This word definitely sounds hateful. Say it a few times; you'll hear what I mean. It's probably not a word that Bella's sweet Gran says too often. You learned a bunch of great synonyms for *loathe* when you had the word *despise* in Group 10: abhor, detest, disdain, scorn.

8. **Infinitesimally** (p. 103) means *an extremely small amount.* You might think that *infinitesimal* should mean an extremely large amount, like *infinite,* but the *-simal* makes it not infinite but *infinith,* meaning broken down into infinite pieces, each being miniscule.

Synonyms: Select the word or phrase whose meaning is closest to the word in capital letters.

1. LOATHE
   A. qualify
   B. vacillate
   C. abhor
   D. reproach
   E. censor

2. SAGACIOUS
   A. convulsive
   B. prudent
   C. abstruse
   D. ubiquitous
   E. finite

3. OMINOUS
   A. foreboding
   B. sterile
   C. astute
   D. infinitesimal
   E. offhand

4. STERILE
   A. uncontaminated
   B. loathsome
   C. lugubrious
   D. lucid
   E. coherent

Analogies: Select the answer choice that best completes the meaning of the sentence.

5. Microscope is to scientist as
   A. sterile is to hospital
   B. scrawl is to animator
   C. lancet is to surgeon
   D. niche is to teacher
   E. stipulation is to arachnophobe

6. Sage is to shrewd as
   A. doctor is to glum
   B. enigma is to cryptic
   C. woolgatherer is to histrionic
   D. pariah is to verbose
   E. gawker is to inconsequential

Sentence Completions: Choose the word that, when inserted in the sentence, best fits the meaning of the sentence as a whole.

7. Villagers had come to trust and respect Genevieve's prudent counsel and often sought her out for these _____ opinions.
   A. ominous
   B. verbose
   C. loathsome
   D. sagacious
   E. sterile

8. Even a(n) _____ hospital room must have infinitesimal amounts of bacteria still present.
   A. shrewd
   B. miffed
   C. impenetrable
   D. transcending
   E. sterile

1. **C.** *Loathe* and *abhor* both mean *hate*. *Qualify* means *to lessen,* *vacillate* means *waver,* *reproach* means *scold,* and *censor* means *cut inappropriate parts of a work of art.*

2. **B.** *Sagacious* and *prudent* both mean *wise.* If you did not initially make the link to the word *prudent,* then use the process of elimination. *Convulsive* means *with sudden movement, abstruse* means *puzzling* (notice the connection to your vocab word *abstract,* which means *dealing with ideas*), *ubiquitous* means *ever-present,* and *finite* means *limited.*

3. **A.** *Ominous* (and *foreboding*) mean *threatening.* *Fore-* means *in front* or *beforehand,* like the foreword in a book, and *-bode* means *predict.* So, *forebode* is *predict (something threatening) beforehand!*

4. **A.** *Sterile* means *totally clean or uncontaminated.* *Loathsome* means *hateful,* *lugubrious* means *glum, lucid* means *clear,* and *coherent* also means *clear.*

5. **C.** "A microscope is used by a scientist."
   A. A sterile is used by a hospital . . . no, that makes no sense, though a hospital is sterile.
   B. A scrawl (messy writing) is used by an animator . . . no, that makes no sense.
   C. A lancet (surgical knife) is used by a surgeon . . . perfect!
   D. A niche (special role) is used by a teacher . . . no.
   E. A stipulation (requirement) is used by an arachnophobe (person afraid of spiders) . . . no.

6. **B.** "A sage is shrewd."
   A. A doctor is glum (sad) . . . no, not necessarily. If you have to tell a long story to connect the words in an answer choice, then it is not the right answer.
   B. An enigma is cryptic . . . yes, a mystery is mysterious.
   C. A woolgatherer (daydreamer) is histrionic (dramatic) . . . no, not necessarily.
   D. A pariah (outcast) is verbose (talkative) . . . no.
   E. A gawker (person who stares) is inconsequential (unimportant) . . . no, not necessarily.

7. **D.** "Villagers had come to trust and respect Genevieve's prudent counsel and often sought her out for these *prudent/wise* opinions."
   Sagacious and *prudent* both mean *wise.* Watch out for choice B; she may or may not have been *verbose* (talkative), but the sentence only offers evidence that she was wise.

8. **E.** "Even a(n) *bacteria-free* hospital room must have infinitesimal amounts of bacteria still present."
   Sterile means *bacteria-free.* Choice C, *impenetrable,* almost works. But it does not fit nearly as well as *sterile.* The sentence does not indicate that the bacteria is breaking into the building, James Bond–style, only that it is *still* present.

Group 18

Appeasement

Find each of the following words on the *Twilight* page number provided. Based on the way each word is used in the book, guess at its definition.

1. **Veered** (p. 103) might mean _____

_____

2. **Indignant** (p. 103) might mean _____

_____

3. **Reproachful** (p. 105) might mean _____

_____

4. **Verified** (p. 107) might mean _____

_____

5. **Malice** (p. 112) might mean _____

_____

6. **Scornfully** (p. 113) might mean _____

_____

7. **Appeased** (p. 114) might mean _____

_____

8. **Austere** (p. 115) might mean _____

_____

Let's see how you did. Check your answers, write the exact definitions, and reread the sentence in *Twilight* where each word appears. Then complete the drills.

1. **Veered** (p. 103) means *switched direction suddenly,* like swerving your bike to avoid a pothole. What word did you learn that has the same meaning? Anyone, anyone? That's right, *wheeling* from Group 14 means *turning suddenly.*

2. **Indignant** (p. 103) means *angry or resentful about unfair treatment.* Synonym: piqued.

3. **Reproachful** (p. 105) means *scolding.* You saw this word as a less extreme version of *condemn* in Group 5. Here are the other synonyms again: censure (more harshly criticize), denounce, rebuke, reprove. You can also add the words *reprimand* and *admonish.*

4. **Verified** (p. 107) means *confirmed. Veri-* refers to *truth,* as in *veracity,* which means *truthfulness.*

5. **Malice** (p. 112) means *ill will.* It's like hatred, but with a plan to do something bad—to be malicious. In fact, *mal-* means *bad,* like *malodorous* (a *bad* smell), *malcontent* (a person with *bad* contentment—a grouch), and *malnourished* (*badly* nourished—undernourished). Synonym: malevolence.

6. **Scornfully** (p. 113) means *with resentment or mocking.* You learned the word *scorn* back in Group 10 as a synonym for *despise.* The end of the word, *-fully,* just means *full of,* so *scornfully* means *full of scorn.* Synonyms: contemptuously, derisively, disdainfully.

7. **Appeased** (p. 114) means *satisfied* or *pleased,* usually from getting what one wants, like Jess getting to sit close to Mike. The SAT absolutely **loves** using synonyms for *appeased*—perhaps they are more fun to use than synonyms for *disappointed* or *hateful.* Synonyms: alleviate, ameliorate, assuage, conciliate, mollify, pacify, palliate (relieve, but not cure), placate.

8. **Austere** (p. 115) means *harsh, very strict,* or *very plain.* Synonyms: severe, stark.

Synonyms: Select the word or phrase whose meaning is closest to the word in capital letters.

1. PIQUED
   A. veering
   B. assuaged
   C. conciliated
   D. resentful
   E. alleviated

2. MALICE
   A. nobility
   B. malevolence
   C. veracity
   D. prudence
   E. abstraction

3. VERITY
   A. malice
   B. austerity
   C. truth
   D. sterility
   E. vacillation

4. APPEASE
   A. veer
   B. disparage
   C. befuddle
   D. wheel
   E. mollify

Analogies: Select the answer choice that best completes the meaning of the sentence.

5. Indignant is to malicious as
   A. reproachful is to condemning
   B. ominous is to menacing
   C. infinitesimal is to tiny
   D. sterile is to boring
   E. recondite is to arcane

6. Veer is to converge as
   A. wheel is to congregate
   B. broach is to evade
   C. flounder is to lance
   D. lumber is to convulse
   E. flit is to loathe

Sentence Completions: Choose the word that, when inserted in the sentence, <u>best</u> fits the meaning of the sentence as a whole.

7. While not curing the disease entirely, certain medications can at least serve as a(n) _____ and relieve many of the symptoms.
   A. austerity
   B. palliative
   C. cure
   D. aversion
   E. stipulation

8. Jacob's earnest apology had a positive effect, his boss seemed greatly _____ and ready to forget Jacob's tardiness.
   A. placated
   B. scornful
   C. indignant
   D. veering
   E. malevolent

1. **D.** *Piqued* means *resentful*. *Veering* means *swerving*. *Assuaged, conciliated,* and *alleviated* all mean *soothed*.
2. **B.** *Malice* means *ill will*. *Malevolence* also means *ill will*. This word reeks of ill will; it even sounds like the word *violence*. *Veracity* means *truth*, *prudence* means *sensibleness*, and *abstraction* means *thought*.
3. **C.** *Verity* means *truth*. *Austerity* means *harshness*, *sterility* means *cleanness*, and *vacillation* means *fluctuation*.
4. **E.** *Appease* sounds like *please*, which is cool since it means *soothe, satisfy,* or *please,* such as Edward's answer did not *appease* Bella's curiosity. *Mollify* also means *soothe*. *Veer* means *swerve, disparage* means *mock, befuddle* means *confuse,* and *wheel* means *swerve*.
5. **A.** "Indignant (resentful) is less extreme than malicious (harmful)."
   - (A.) Reproachful (scolding) is less extreme than condemning (sharply criticizing) . . . yes.
   - B. Ominous is less extreme than menacing . . . no, they both mean *threatening*.
   - C. Infinitesimal is less extreme than tiny . . . no, they mean the same thing.
   - D. Sterile is less extreme than boring . . . no, *sterile* can mean *boring*.
   - E. Recondite is less extreme than arcane . . . no, they both mean *mysterious*.
6. **A.** "You might veer (change direction) in order to converge (come together)."
   - (A.) You might wheel (change direction) in order to congregate (come together) . . . yes.
   - B. You might broach (bring up a topic) in order to evade (avoid) . . . no, the opposite.
   - C. You might flounder (struggle) in order to lance (pierce) . . . no, they are unrelated.
   - D. You might lumber (walk awkwardly) in order to convulse (contort) . . . no, they are unrelated.
   - E. You might flit (move quickly) in order to loathe (hate) . . . no, they are unrelated.
7. **B.** "While not curing the disease entirely, certain medications can at least serve as a(n) <u>reliever</u> and relieve many of the symptoms."
   Palliative means *something that provides relief but does not cure*.
8. **A.** "Jacob's earnest apology had a positive effect, his boss seemed greatly <u>soothed</u> and ready to forget Jacob's tardiness."
   Placated means *soothed*.

Ceaseless Questions

Find each of the following words on the *Twilight* page number provided. Based on the way each word is used in the book, guess at its definition.

1. **Solitary** (p. 115) might mean _____

_____

2. **Briny** (p. 115) might mean _____

_____

3. **Bouquets** (p. 117) might mean _____

_____

4. **Anemones** (p. 117) might mean _____

_____

5. **Undulated** (p. 117) might mean _____

_____

6. **Ceaselessly** (p. 117) might mean _____

_____

7. **Nape** (p. 119) might mean _____

_____

8. **Russet** (p. 119) might mean _____

_____

1. **Solitary** (p. 115) means *alone*. That's easy to remember since the game solitaire is for one person. Synonym: reclusive.

2. **Briny** (p. 115) means *salty*.

3. **Bouquets** (p. 117) means *beautiful groupings*. In this case it refers to anemones, but usually it refers to flowers, like in the TV show *House, M.D.*, when Dr. Cameron says, "What do you think House would send, the 'Gentle Comfort' arrangement, or the 'Warm Thoughts' **bouquet?** I mean, if he wasn't an . . ." (Fox, *Birthmarks,* 2008)

4. **Anemones** (p. 117) is short for *sea anemones,* which are sea animals that attach to rocks or coral. They have tentacles that undulate, as you are about to find out . . .

5. **Undulated** (p. 117) means *moved in a flowing, wavelike motion.* A lithe belly dancer might undulate.

6. **Ceaselessly** (p. 117) means *endlessly. Cease* means *end,* as in the enemies reached a ceasefire. Synonyms: eternally, incessantly, interminably (*in* means *not,* and *termin* refers to *end*), relentlessly.

7. **Nape** (p. 119) means *back,* usually of the neck.

8. **Russet** (p. 119) means *reddish-brown.* You've learned three colors so far: *auburn* (reddish-brown, usually for hair), *ocher* (brownish-yellow), and now *russet* (reddish-brown). Notice that auburn and russet are both reddish-brown. That's Edward's hair and Jacob's skin—so at least that's one thing that they have in common!

Synonyms: Select the word or phrase whose meaning is closest to the word in capital letters.

1. RELENTLESS
   - A. solitary
   - B. ceaseless
   - C. lawless
   - D. indignant
   - E. verified

2. UNDULATE
   - A. appease
   - B. mollify
   - C. placate
   - D. assuage
   - E. ripple

3. SOLITARY
   - A. reclusive
   - B. briny
   - C. incessant
   - D. interminable
   - E. eternal

4. CEASE
   - A. veer
   - B. terminate
   - C. reproach
   - D. abhor
   - E. qualify

Analogies: Select the answer choice that best completes the meaning of the sentence.

5. Anemone is to briny as
   - A. nape is to russet
   - B. patron is to finite
   - C. vampire is to surreptitious
   - D. novelty is to nostalgic
   - E. niche is to wary

6. Solitary is to communal as
   - A. incessant is to finite
   - B. russet is to ocher
   - C. bouquet is to flowers
   - D. undulate is to dance
   - E. nape is to eaves

Sentence Completions: Choose the word that, when inserted in the sentence, best fits the meaning of the sentence as a whole.

7. With sinuous grace, the waves _____ across the surface of the ocean toward shore.
   - A. ceased
   - B. verified
   - C. undulated
   - D. scorned
   - E. assuaged

8. The child tried _____ to pick up her pet rabbit, and finally, after many attempts, lifted him by the nape of his neck.
   - A. solitarily
   - B. austerely
   - C. loathingly
   - D. sagely
   - E. relentlessly

1. **B.** *Relentless* and *ceaseless* mean *endless,* since *relent* and *cease* both
mean *end. Solitary* means *alone, indignant* means *resentful,* and
verified means *confirmed.*
2. **E.** *Undulate* means *move in a wavelike way,* like a belly dancer.
That's also what *ripple* means, like the ripples on a lake after
Charlie casts his fishing line. *Appease, mollify, placate,* and *assuage*
all mean *satisfy.*
3. **A.** *Solitary* and *reclusive* mean *alone. Briny* means *salty. Incessant,*
interminable, and *eternal* mean *endless.*
4. **B.** *Cease* means *end,* that's why *ceaseless* means *endless* or *without an*
end. Terminate also means *end. Veer* means *swerve, reproach* means
scold, abhor means *hate,* and *qualify* means *lessen.*
5. **C.** "An anemone lives in a briny (salty) environment."
   A . A nape (back, usually of the neck) lives in a russet (reddish-
   brown) environment . . . no.
   B . A patron (supporter) lives in a finite (limited) environment . . . no.
   C . A vampire lives in a surreptitious (secretive) environment . . .
   yes, unless they want to be discovered! Okay that one was tough
   and maybe lame, and a standardized test would never use it, but
   it was fun and good practice using the process of elimination.
   D . A novelty (new thing) lives in a nostalgic (sentimental)
   environment . . . no.
   E . A niche (appropriate position) lives in a wary (cautious)
   environment . . . no.
6. **A.** "Solitary (alone) is the opposite of communal (part of a group)."
   A . Incessant (endless) is the opposite of finite (limited) . . . yes.
   B . Russet (reddish-brown) is the opposite of ocher (brownish-
   yellow) . . . no, they're similar.
   C . Bouquet is the opposite of flowers . . . no, it contains
   flowers.
   D . Undulate (move like a wave) is the opposite of dance . . . no.
   E . Nape (back, usually of the neck) is the opposite of eaves
   (where the roof overhangs the walls) . . . no.
7. **C.** "With sinuous grace, the waves *moved/waved* across the surface
   of the ocean toward shore."
   Undulated means *flowed in a wavelike motion.*
8. **E.** "The child tried *many attempts* to pick up her pet rabbit, and
   finally, after many attempts, lifted him by the nape of his neck."
   Relentlessly means *endlessly.*

An Alluring Menace

Find each of the following words on the *Twilight* page number provided. Based on the way each word is used in the book, guess at its definition.

1. **Insolent** (p. 121) might mean _____

    _____

2. **Condescendingly** (p. 121) might mean _____

    _____

3. **Multihued** (p. 122) might mean _____

    _____

4. **Alluring** (p. 123) might mean _____

    _____

5. **Attenuated** (p. 123) might mean _____

    _____

6. **Deliberately** (p. 125) might mean _____

    _____

7. **Menace** (p. 125) might mean _____

    _____

8. **Inept** (p. 127) might mean _____

    _____

Let's see how you did. Check your answers, write the exact definitions,
and reread the sentence in *Twilight* where each word appears. Then
complete the drills.

1. **Insolent** (p. 121) means *rudely or arrogantly disrespectful.* Synonyms:
   audacious, cheeky, impertinent, impudent, sassy. Professor Snape
   often complains to Dumbledore of Harry Potter's **insolence.** And,
   in group therapy, Dr. Evil describes, "My childhood was typical.
   Summers in Rangoon, luge lessons. In the spring we'd make meat
   helmets. When I was **insolent** I was placed in a burlap bag and
   beaten with reeds—pretty standard really." (New Line Cinema,
   Austin Powers: International Man of Mystery, 1997)

2. **Condescendingly** (p. 121) means *with superiority.* That makes
   sense since *con-* means *with* (just like in Spanish) and *descend*
   means *down*—like looking down on someone. This word means
   the same as *patronizingly,* from Group 12.

3. **Multihued** (p. 122) means *many colored,* since *multi-* means *many,*
   and *hue* means *color.*

4. **Alluring** (p. 123) means *appealing and charming.*

5. **Attenuated** (p. 123) means *thinned* or *lessened.* It can also mean
   soothed, just like *alleviate, ameliorate, assuage, conciliate, mollify, pacify,
   palliate,* and *placate.*

6. **Deliberately** (p. 125) means *on purpose.* It can also mean *with care,*
   as opposed to *rushed* or *hasty.* Sometimes the SAT or ACT uses the
   latter meaning, which throws some students who don't expect it.

7. **Menace** (p. 125) means *threat.* Remember that *menacing* is a
   synonym for *ominous.* These words come up a lot in *Twilight,*
   which makes sense, actually, in a book about someone dating a
   vampire.

8. **Inept** (p. 127) means *clumsy* or *incompetent,* as opposed to say,
   Edward, who is graceful and skilled at everything. The opposite of
   inept is *adroit* (dexterous and skilled).

Synonyms: Select the word or phrase whose meaning is closest to the word in capital letters.

Drills

1. INSOLENT
   A. alluring
   B. multihued
   C. impertinent
   D. attenuated
   E. ominous

2. ALLURING
   A. briny
   B. ceaseless
   C. appealing
   D. russet
   E. inept

3. MENACING
   A. condescending
   B. patronizing
   C. inept
   D. ominous
   E. solitary

4. DELIBERATE
   A. attenuated
   B. careful
   C. menacing
   D. solitary
   E. indignant

Analogies: Select the answer choice that best completes the meaning of the sentence.

5. Insolent is to respect as
   A. dubious is to doubt
   B. deliberate is to haste
   C. wry is to prudence
   D. euphoric is to elation
   E. petulant is to irritation

6. Russet is to hue as
   A. auburn is to tint
   B. transparent is to opaque
   C. ocher is to scrawl
   D. inexplicable is to error
   E. menace is to allure

Sentence Completions: Choose the word that, when inserted in the sentence, best fits the meaning of the sentence as a whole.

7. Most clowns can juggle, dance, and perform simple acrobatics; these _____ performers have many talents.
   A. adroit
   B. menacing
   C. inept
   D. condescending
   E. insolent

8. Mr. Peabody did not care for Mel's _____ tone and planned a suitable reprimand.
   A. alluring
   B. attenuated
   C. pacifying
   D. impudent
   E. multihued

1. **C.** *Insolent* means *disrespectful*. That's also what *impertinent* means. That makes sense since *im-* means *not*, and *pertinent* means *appropriate*, so impertinent behavior is inappropriate or rude!

2. **C.** *Alluring* means *appealing*. *Briny* means *salty*, *ceaseless* means *endless*, *russet* means *reddish-brown*, and *inept* means *unskilled*.

3. **D.** *Menacing* means *threatening*. That's also what *ominous* means. *Condescending* and *patronizing* mean *looking down on*. And *solitary* means *alone*.

4. **B.** *Deliberate* means *on purpose* or *careful*. Use the process of elimination—cross off answers that you are sure don't work and choose the best of what's left. *Attenuated* means *thinned* or *soothed*, and *indignant* means *resentful*.

5. **B.** "Someone who is insolent (rude) does not show respect."
   A. Someone who is dubious (doubtful) does not show doubt . . . no, they do.
   (B.) Someone who is deliberate (intentional) does not show haste (rushing) . . . true.
   C. Someone who is wry (using dry humor) does not show prudence (wisdom) . . . no.
   D. Someone who is euphoric (thrilled) does not show elation (happiness) . . . no.
   E. Someone who is petulant (irritable) does not show irritation . . . no!

6. **A.** "Russet (reddish-brown) is a type of hue (color)."
   (A.) Auburn (reddish-brown) is a type of tint (shade) . . . yes.
   B. Transparent (see-through) is a type of opaque (solid/not see-through) . . . no.
   C. Ocher (brownish-yellow) is a type of scrawl (messy writing) . . . no.
   D. Inexplicable (not explainable) is a type of error . . . no.
   E. Menace (threat) is a type of allure (appeal) . . . no, well, unless maybe you're Bella!

7. **A.** "Most clowns can juggle, dance, and perform simple acrobatics; these _talented/versatile_ performers have many talents."
   Adroit means *dexterous and skilled*. A surprising number of people have a fear of clowns; even so, Choice B, *menacing*, is not the correct answer.

8. **D.** "Mr. Peabody did not care for Mel's _rude_ tone and planned a suitable reprimand."
   Impudent means *rude*.

Quiz 4

I. Let's review some of the words that you've seen in Groups 16–20. Match each of the following words to the correct definition or synonym on the right. Then check the solutions on page 171.

1. Flippant	A. Outcast
2. Vacillating	B. Offhand
3. Pariah	C. Resentful
4. Sagacious	D. Wavering
5. Abhor	E. Assuage
6. Indignant	F. Harsh
7. Reproach	G. Wise
8. Malice	H. Loathe
9. Placate	I. Solitary
10. Austere	J. Careful
11. Reclusive	K. Scold
12. Undulate	L. Ill will
13. Deliberate	M. Patronize
14. Condescend	N. Move in a smooth-flowing motion
15. Menace	O. Threat

II. Let's review several of the word parts that you've seen in Groups 16–20. Match each of the following word parts to the correct definition or synonym on the right. Then check the solutions on page 171.

16. Micro-	A. Not
17. Scope-	B. With
18. Phone-	C. Bad
19. Im-	D. Instrument for observing
20. Mal-	E. Small
21. Con-	F. Instrument that works with sound

Review

Match each group of synonyms to its general meaning. Then check the solutions on page 171.

1. Agile
   Lissome
   Lithe
   Nimble
   Supple

   A. Excessively proud

2. Clandestine
   Covert
   Furtive
   Surreptitious

   B. Hate

3. Ecstatic
   Elated
   Euphoric
   Jubilant
   Rapturous

   C. Flexible and graceful

4. Apprehensive
   Cagy
   Circumspect
   Vigilant
   Wary

   D. Secretive

5. Arrogant
   Bombastic
   Haughty
   Smug

   E. Thrilled

6. Abhor
   Despise
   Detest
   Disdain
   Loathe
   Scorn

   F. Cautious

Judicious Camaraderie?

Find each of the following words on the *Twilight* page number provided. Based on the way each word is used in the book, guess at its definition.

1. **Camaraderie** (p. 128) might mean _____

   _____

2. **Blaring** (p. 130) might mean _____

   _____

3. **Plaits** (p. 132) might mean _____

   _____

4. **Dredged up** (p. 132) might mean _____

   _____

5. **Substandard** (p. 132) might mean _____

   _____

6. **Abhorred** (p. 133) might mean _____

   _____

7. **Affidavits** (p. 133) might mean _____

   _____

8. **Judicial** (p. 134) might mean _____

   _____

Let's see how you did. Check your answers, write the exact definitions, and reread the sentence in *Twilight* where each word appears. Then complete the drills.

1. **Camaraderie** (p. 128) means *warmth and friendship.* It actually comes from the Spanish word *camarada* for *roommate.* If you've ever shared a room with someone, you know that you can become pretty close. Actually, Bella and Edward do sorta share a room, but don't tell Charlie . . . or Jacob or Mike for that matter. Synonym: amity.

2. **Blaring** (p. 130) means *loud and harsh.*

3. **Plaits** (p. 132) means *interlaced strands.* Few people know this word, but you can get it in the context of the paragraph. Figuring out the meaning of a word by reading the words and sentences around it is a great skill to practice. Tests such as the ACT and GED Science sections are not testing whether you've memorized science terms; they always define the terms in the passage!

4. **Dredged up** (p. 132) means *brought up.*

5. **Substandard** (p. 132) means *below the standard. Sub-* means *under* or *below,* as in *submarine* (under water). *Sub-* can also mean *next,* as in *subsequent* (next in the sequence).

6. **Abhorred** (p. 133) means *hated.* You saw this word as a synonym for *despise* in Group 10 and *loathe* in Group 17. The other synonyms were *detest, disdain,* and *scorn.*

7. **Affidavits** (p. 133) means *written statements sworn under oath,* usually for use in court.

8. **Judicial** (p. 134) means *of a court* or *relating to judgment.* The related word *judicious* means *wise* or *prudent.* You learned the word *prudent* in Group 15. Okay, quick quiz: Who said on page 84 of *Twilight,* "It would be more . . . *prudent* for you not to be my friend"? Who was he talking to, and why did he say it?

Synonyms: Select the word or phrase whose meaning is closest to the word in capital letters.

1. AMITY
   A. plaits
   B. abhorrence
   C. camaraderie
   D. affidavits
   E. allure

2. SUBSTANDARD
   A. noble
   B. judicial
   C. pale
   D. omnipresent
   E. inferior

3. ABHOR
   A. dredge
   B. loathe
   C. blare
   D. judge
   E. supplement

4. AFFIDAVITS
   A. plaits
   B. hues
   C. brine
   D. legal documents
   E. anemones

Analogies: Select the answer choice that best completes the meaning of the sentence.

5. Plaits is to auburn as
   A. lancet is to hue
   B. camaraderie is to ocher
   C. skin is to russet
   D. menace is to burgundy
   E. insolence is to red

6. Judicious is to foolish as
   A. chaos is to bedlam
   B. blaring is to muted
   C. detest is to despise
   D. solitary is to alone
   E. cease is to terminate

Sentence Completions: Choose the word or phrase that, when inserted in the sentence, <u>best</u> fits the meaning of the sentence as a whole.

7. After spending two months living in a van and traveling the country, Bill and Ted's friendship had deepened and they shared a genuine _____.
   A. loathing
   B. vacillation
   C. camaraderie
   D. petulance
   E. jubilation

8. Max was surprised that seeing his ex-girlfriend, even after three months, would _____ so many feelings.
   A. allure
   B. veer out
   C. blare out
   D. dredge up
   E. mute

1. **C.** *Amity* and *camaraderie* mean *friendship*. The word *amity* is easy to remember—it's related to the Spanish word *amigo* and the French word *ami* meaning *friend*. *Plaits* means *interlaced strands of hair, abhorrence* means *hatred, affidavits* are *legal documents,* and *allure* means *appeal*.

2. **E.** *Substandard* and *inferior* mean *below standard*. *Noble* means *dignified, judicial* means *relating to judgment,* and *omnipresent* means *widespread*.

3. **B.** *Abhor* and *loathe* both mean *hate*. *Dredge* means *bring (up), blare* means *sound harshly,* and *supplement* means *add to complete*.

4. **D.** *Affidavits* means *legal documents*. *Hues* are *colors, brine* means *salt,* and *anemones* are *lovely sea creatures*.

5. **C.** "Plaits could be auburn colored."
   A. Lancet (surgical knife) could be hue (color) colored . . . no, that makes no sense.
   B. Camaraderie (friendship) could be ocher (brownish-yellow) colored . . . no, that makes no sense.
   C. Skin could be russet colored . . . yes, hello Jacob.
   D. Menace (threat) could be burgundy (deep red) colored . . . no, unless they are deep red vampire eyes—that's a threat.
   E. Insolence (rudeness) could be red colored . . . no, that makes no sense.

6. **B.** "Judicious is the opposite of foolish."
   A. Chaos is the opposite of bedlam . . . no, they are synonyms.
   B. Blaring is the opposite of muted . . . yes, loud is the opposite of quiet.
   C. Detest is the opposite of despise . . . no, they both mean *hate*.
   D. Solitary is the opposite of alone . . . no, they are synonyms.
   E. Cease is the opposite of terminate . . . no, they both mean *end*.

7. **C.** "After spending two months living in a van and traveling the country, Bill and Ted's friendship had deepened and they shared a genuine *friendship*."
   Camaraderie means *friendship*. *Petulance* means *irritation*. They probably felt that, too, after months in a van together, but the sentence is definitely about the friendship.

8. **D.** "Max was surprised that seeing his ex-girlfriend, even after three months, would *bring up* so many feelings."
   Dredge up means *bring up*.

Group 22
Plausible Explanations?

Find each of the following words on the *Twilight* page number provided. Based on the way each word is used in the book, guess at its definition.

1. **Plausible** (p. 134) might mean _____
_____

2. **Constructs** (p. 134) might mean _____
_____

3. **Mortality** (p. 134) might mean _____
_____

4. **Infidelity** (p. 134) might mean _____
_____

5. **Mortal** (p. 135) might mean _____
_____

6. **Sodden** (p. 135) might mean _____
_____

7. **Encroaching** (p. 136) might mean _____
_____

8. **Ebb** (p. 136) might mean _____
_____

90

Let's see how you did. Check your answers, write the exact definitions, and reread the sentence in *Twilight* where each word appears. Then complete the drills.

1. **Plausible** (p. 134) means *reasonable, probable,* or *believable.* Synonyms: credible, feasible. Incidentally, since *in-* means *not, incredible* means *not credible* or *not believable.*

2. **Constructs** (p. 134) means *theories, usually created without much solid evidence.* It comes from the word *construct,* as in *to build the theory.*

3. **Mortality** (p. 134) means *death* or *subject to death.* The fact that humans are mortal is just a fancy way of saying that humans eventually die. Vampires, on the other hand, do not die of old age and are therefore *immortal* (not mortal). Synonym for *mortal: transient.* Remember that you had *intransience* as a synonym for *permanence* in Group 1.

4. **Infidelity** (p. 134) means *unfaithfulness to a partner.* You already know that *in-* means *not,* and since *-fidel* refers to *faithful,* you can see why *infidelity* means *unfaithfulness. Fidelity* means *trustworthiness,* that's why banks use names like Fidelity National Bank.

5. **Mortal** (p. 135) means *deadly* or *fatal,* just like *mortality* means *death* or *subject to death. Mortal* comes from the root *mort-,* which means *death.* That's a lot of death words. You have also had a plethora of *threat* words, like *ominous* and *menacing.* What did you expect from a vampire book?!

6. **Sodden** (p. 135), like *saturated* from Group 8, means *totally soaked.*

7. **Encroaching** (p. 136) means *intruding* or *advancing.*

8. **Ebb** (p. 136) means *reduce* or *recede.* Synonym: wane. During high tide the waves might *encroach* on your beach blanket, but in low tide the water *ebbs* away.

Synonyms: Select the word or phrase whose meaning is closest to the word in capital letters.

Drills

1. CREDIBLE
   A. mortal
   B. plausible
   C. sodden
   D. ebbing
   E. constructed

2. TRANSIENT
   A. noble
   B. compendious
   C. plausible
   D. faithful
   E. mortal

3. INFIDELITY
   A. disloyalty
   B. encroachment
   C. camaraderie
   D. amity
   E. affidavits

4. CONSTRUCT
   A. plausible
   B. vigorous
   C. theory
   D. encroach
   E. ebb

Analogies: Select the answer choice that best completes the meaning of the sentence.

5. Sodden is to saturated as
   A. ebbing is to advancing
   B. plausible is to impossible
   C. stipulate is to request
   D. encroaching is to advancing
   E. infidelity is to loyalty

6. Wane is to encroach as
   A. ebb is to retreat
   B. wheel is to veer
   C. dredge is to bury
   D. broach is to dredge
   E. substandard is to inferior

Sentence Completions: Choose the word that, when inserted in the sentence, <u>best</u> fits the meaning of the sentence as a whole.

7. Aretha felt that her neighbor's oak tree was _____ on the boundary of her yard, and she planned to ask him to cut it back.
   A. encroaching
   B. ebbing
   C. mortally
   D. faithfully
   E. constructing

8. A bank must project an air of _____ for customers to trust their money to the institution.
   A. mortality
   B. opacity
   C. fidelity
   D. transience
   E. insolence

1. **B.** *Credible* and *plausible* mean *believable*. *Cred-* refers to *believe,* as in *credential* (a qualification that makes someone believable) and *creed* (a system of beliefs).

2. **E.** *Transient* means *temporary* or *impermanent*. Remember from *translucent* in Group 2 that *trans-* means *across,* so *transient* refers to *someone or something moving across* and *not staying permanently*. That's why *transient* means *mortal* (just passing through), whereas *intransient* means *immortal* (here to stay).

3. **A.** *Infidelity* means *disloyalty*. *Encroachment* means *intrusion* or *a gradual advancing*. *Camaraderie* and *amity* mean *friendship,* and *affidavits* are *legal documents*.

4. **C.** *Construct* means *theory*. Of course, it also means *build,* but that's not a choice. This is a great example of a word with two meanings that the SAT, ACT, GED, or SSAT might use in a reading comprehension question. The question would offer *build* and *theory* as answers, and you would have to decide how it was used in the context of the passage. On those questions, always reread a few sentences before and a few sentences after the line where the word appears in the passage.

5. **D.** "Sodden is a synonym for saturated."
   A. Ebbing is a synonym for advancing . . . no, they are opposites.
   B. Plausible is a synonym for impossible . . . no, they are opposites.
   C. Stipulate is a synonym for request . . . no, *stipulate* means *require,* not request.
   D. Encroaching is a synonym for advancing . . . yes.
   E. Infidelity is a synonym for loyalty . . . no, they are opposites.

6. **C.** "Wane (recede) is the opposite of encroach (advance)."
   A. Ebb is the opposite of retreat . . . no, they are synonyms.
   B. Wheel is the opposite of veer . . . no, they both mean *turn quickly.*
   C. Dredge is the opposite of bury . . . yes, *dredge* means *dig up.*
   D. Broach is the opposite of dredge . . . no, they are similar.
   E. Substandard is the opposite of inferior . . . no, they are synonyms.

7. **A.** "Aretha felt that her neighbor's oak tree was <u>advancing</u> on the boundary of her yard, and she planned to ask him to cut it back." *Encroaching* means *intruding* or *advancing*.

8. **C.** "A bank must project an air of <u>trust</u> for customers to trust their money to the institution." *Fidelity* means *faithfulness,* which is pretty close to *trust*. Remember that *opacity* means that *light cannot pass through, transience* means *impermanence,* and *insolence* means *rudeness*.

Morbid Thoughts

Find each of the following words on the *Twilight* page number provided. Based on the way each word is used in the book, guess at its definition.

1. **Morbid** (p. 137) might mean _____

   _____

2. **Cadences** (p. 138) might mean _____

   _____

3. **Incredulous** (p. 138) might mean _____

   _____

4. **Despair** (p. 139) might mean _____

   _____

5. **Sinister** (p. 139) might mean _____

   _____

6. **Concealment** (p. 139) might mean _____

   _____

7. **Serene** (p. 140) might mean _____

   _____

8. **Tainted** (p. 140) might mean _____

   _____

Let's see how you did. Check your answers, write the exact definitions, and reread the sentence in *Twilight* where each word appears. Then complete the drills.

1. **Morbid** (p. 137) means *gloomy and disturbing*. Synonyms: macabre, morose.

2. **Cadences** (p. 138) means *rhythms*.

3. **Incredulous** (p. 138) means *unbelieving*. Remember from Group 22 that *cred-* refers to *believe,* and of course *in-* means *not,* so you can see why *incredulous* means *unbelieving* or *doubting*. That reminds me of the word *dubious* that you had in Group 15.

4. **Despair** (p. 139) means *misery or hopelessness*. Synonyms: anguish, desolation, despondency, wretchedness.

5. **Sinister** (p. 139) means *wicked*. Synonyms: baleful, depraved, heinous, impious, iniquitous, malevolent, menacing, nefarious, pernicious. If you search for movies and television shows that contain the word *sinister,* you'll find lots of vampire shows: *Buffy the Vampire Slayer, The Lost Boys, Interview with the Vampire,* and even *Count Duckula.* Aside from the vegetarians, vampires can be pretty sinister!

6. **Concealment** (p. 139) means *hiding*.

7. **Serene** (p. 140) means *calm and peaceful*. How can you remember this word? How about *Gossip Girl*'s Serena van der Woodsen. Though she's not **always** calm and tranquil, things usually go her way without too much of a fuss or fight. Synonyms: placid, tranquil.

8. **Tainted** (p. 140) means *contaminated*.

Synonyms: Select the word or phrase whose meaning is closest to the word in capital letters.

Drills

1. MORBID
   A. concealed
   B. gloomy
   C. serene
   D. dubious
   E. plausible

2. CADENCE
   A. infidelity
   B. mortality
   C. rhythm
   D. blare
   E. amity

3. INCREDULOUS
   A. morbid
   B. literal
   C. dubious
   D. heinous
   E. nefarious

4. PERNICIOUS
   A. wicked
   B. tainted
   C. concealed
   D. incredulous
   E. cadenced

Analogies: Select the answer choice that best completes the meaning of the sentence.

5. Tranquil is to serene as
   A. cadence is to vacillation
   B. serenity is to hostility
   C. placid is to impious
   D. morbid is to macabre
   E. tainted is to malevolent

6. Toxin is to tainted as
   A. concealment is to hidden
   B. despair is to appeased
   C. attenuation is to thicker
   D. undulation is to still
   E. relentless is to cease

Sentence Completions: Choose the word that, when inserted in the sentence, <u>best</u> fits the meaning of the sentence as a whole.

7. Concealed behind a tree, the villain watched and let out a _____ laugh.
   A. sodden
   B. encroaching
   C. judicial
   D. sinister
   E. multihued

8. The rhythm of the music, with its hypnotic _____, inspired listeners to dance.
   A. taint
   B. cadence
   C. ebb
   D. blare
   E. veering

1. **B.** *Morbid* means *gloomy.* *Concealed* means *hidden, serene* means
   calm, dubious means *doubtful,* and *plausible* means *believable.*
2. **C.** *Cadence* means *rhythm.* *Infidelity* means *disloyalty, mortality*
   means *humanness, blare* means *loud sound* (not necessarily with
   rhythm), and *amity* means *friendship.*
3. **C.** *Incredulous* means *disbelieving,* so *dubious,* which means *doubtful,* is the
   best answer. If that seems tricky, use the process of elimination. *Literal*
   means *exact,* and *heinous* and *nefarious* are two terrific words for *evil.*
4. **A.** *Pernicious* means *wicked.* *Tainted* means *contaminated* and
   concealed means *hidden.*
5. **D.** "Tranquil means serene."
   - A . Cadence means vacillation . . . no, close though. *Cadence*
     means *rhythm,* and *vacillation* means *waver,* but not
     necessarily with rhythm.
   - B . Serenity means hostility . . . no, peace does not mean
     unfriendliness.
   - C . Placid means impious . . . no, peaceful does not mean wicked.
   - (D.) Morbid means macabre . . . yes, both words mean *very gloomy.*
   - E . Tainted means malevolent . . . no, contaminated does not
     mean spiteful.
6. **A.** "Toxin makes something tainted."
   - (A.) Concealment makes something hidden . . . yes!
   - B . Despair makes something appeased . . . no, sadness does
     not make someone happy.
   - C . Attenuation makes something thicker . . . no, thinning does
     not make something thicker.
   - D . Undulation makes something still . . . no, *undulation* means
     wavelike movement.
   - E . Relentless makes something cease . . . no, *relentless*
     (unending) does not make something end.
7. **D.** "Concealed behind a tree, the villain watched and let out a
   <u>villainous</u> laugh."

   Sinister means *villainous.* This sentence gives less information
   about the blank than most sentence completion questions. When
   this happens, decide if the word should be positive or negative, or
   get a basic feel for the word and then use the process of elimination.
   Especially in this case, it's critical to eliminate choices **only** when you
   are absolutely positive that they don't fit. Then choose the best of the
   remaining choices. *Sodden* means *soaked, encroaching* means *intruding,*
   judicial means *pertaining to courts,* and *multihued* means *multicolored.*
8. **B.** "The rhythm of the music, with its hypnotic <u>rhythm,</u> inspired
   listeners to dance."

   Cadence means *rhythm.* *Blare* relates to sound, but does not
   mean *rhythmic;* it only means *noisy.*

Euphoria

Find each of the following words on the *Twilight* page number provided. Based on the way each word is used in the book, guess at its definition.

1. **By dint of** (p. 142) might mean _____

    _____

2. **Seldom** (p. 142) might mean _____

    _____

3. **Industriously** (p. 142) might mean _____

    _____

4. **Proprietary** (p. 143) might mean _____

    _____

5. **Misogynistic** (p. 143) might mean _____

    _____

6. **Immersed** (p. 144) might mean _____

    _____

7. **Indecisive** (p. 145) might mean _____

    _____

8. **Euphoric** (p. 145) might mean _____

    _____

Let's see how you did. Check your answers, write the exact definitions,
and reread the sentence in *Twilight* where each word appears. Then
complete the drills.

1. **By dint of** (p. 142) means *because of* and is usually used when an
   action requires force, like rolling down the windows on a 1959
   Chevy truck. This phrase actually comes from the word *dent,* such
   as, "Did you make a dent in your English homework?"

2. **Seldom** (p. 142) means *rarely.*

3. **Industriously** (p. 142) means *with focused hard work in mind.* This is
   where the term *industry,* meaning *manufacturing or other branches of
   business activity,* comes from. Synonyms for *industrious:* assiduous,
   conscientious, diligent, sedulous.

4. **Proprietary** (p. 143) means *possessive.* That's easy to remember,
   since basically, *proprietary* refers to *property.*

5. **Misogynistic** (p. 143) means *hating women. Mis-* can refer to *hate.*
   And *-gyn* refers to *women;* that's why a doctor who specializes
   in women's heath (especially reproductive health) is called a
   gynecologist.

6. **Immersed** (p. 144) means *engrossed or submerged.* Literally, it means
   to submerge something in liquid, and figuratively it means to be
   totally preoccupied with something—submerged in it. Remember
   the words *saturated* and *sodden?* If you submerge something in
   liquid, after awhile it might get *saturated* or *sodden.*

7. **Indecisive** (p. 145) means *not decisive* or *unsure.* This is a great
   synonym for *vacillating* from Group 16. Another good synonym is
   irresolute.

8. **Euphoric** (p. 145) means *thrilled.* This was a synonym for *elated* in
   Group 6. The other synonyms were *ecstatic, jubilant,* and *rapturous.*

Synonyms: Select the word or phrase whose meaning is closest to the word in capital letters.

Drills

1. ASSIDUOUS
   A. lazy
   B. diligent
   C. misogynistic
   D. proprietary
   E. ecstatic

2. IRRESOLUTE
   A. ignoble
   B. ineffective
   C. indecisive
   D. insistent
   E. irresponsible

3. EUPHORIC
   A. immersed
   B. morbid
   C. incredulous
   D. depraved
   E. ecstatic

4. INDUSTRIOUS
   A. sinister
   B. pernicious
   C. sedulous
   D. concealed
   E. tainted

Analogies: Select the answer choice that best completes the meaning of the sentence.

5. Industrious is to immersed as
   A. indecisive is to resolute
   B. wavering is to certain
   C. nefarious is to concealed
   D. conscientious is to engrossed
   E. mortal is to sodden

6. Seldom is to perpetual as
   A. compelled is to suspicious
   B. remorseful is to repentant
   C. sodden is to dry
   D. vehement is to fervent
   E. opportune is to auspicious

Sentence Completions: Choose the word that, when inserted in the sentence, <u>best</u> fits the meaning of the sentence as a whole.

7. Unsure of ownership, Meera asked her lawyer if the company had a(n) _____ right to the land on which her building was constructed.
   A. submerged
   B. rapturous
   C. industrious
   D. proprietary
   E. iniquitous

8. Sure that she could help eliminate _____, Aisha fought assiduously for women's rights.
   A. misogyny
   B. indecision
   C. concealment
   D. desolation
   E. constructs

1. **B.** *Assiduous* means *very diligent,* so choice B is the best answer.
   Misogynistic means *hating women, proprietary* means *relating to ownership,* and *ecstatic* means *thrilled.*
2. **C.** *Irresolute* means *uncertain,* so choice C is best. This is a great word to break apart. *Ir-* means *not,* as in *irresponsible,* and *resolute* means *determined. Ignoble* means *not noble.*
3. **E.** *Euphoric* means *thrilled,* as do *ecstatic, elated, jubilant,* and *rapturous. Immersed* means *submerged, morbid* means *gloomy, incredulous* means *doubting,* and *depraved* means *wicked.*
4. **C.** *Industrious* and *sedulous* both mean *diligent and hard working. Sinister* and *pernicious* mean *wicked. Tainted* means *contaminated.*
5. **D.** "An industrious person might get immersed in a task."
   - A. An indecisive person might get resolute in a task . . . no, *resolute* means *certain.*
   - B. A wavering person might get certain in a task . . . no, *wavering* means *uncertain.*
   - C. A nefarious (evil) person might get concealed (hidden) in a task . . . no, not necessarily.
   - (D.) A conscientious (diligent) person might get engrossed in a task . . . yes!
   - E. A mortal (human) person might get sodden (soaked) in a task . . . no, not necessarily.
6. **C.** "Seldom (rarely) is the opposite of perpetual (continual)."
   - A. Compelled (obligated) is the opposite of suspicious . . . no.
   - B. Remorseful is the opposite of repentant . . . no, they both mean *regretful.*
   - (C.) Sodden (soaked) is the opposite of dry . . . yes!
   - D. Vehement is the opposite of fervent . . . no, they both mean *passionate.*
   - E. Opportune is the opposite of auspicious . . . no, they both mean *well-timed.*
7. **D.** "Unsure of ownership, Meera asked her lawyer if the company had a(n) <u>ownership</u> right to the land on which her building was constructed."
   Proprietary means *relating to ownership. Industrious* means *diligent, rapturous* means *thrilled,* and *iniquitous* means *wicked.*
8. **A.** "Sure that she could help eliminate <u>lack of women's rights,</u> Aisha fought assiduously for women's rights."
   Misogyny means *hatred of women. Desolation* means *misery,* and *constructs* means *theories.* Several answers might seem to work, but the sentence provides most direct and specific evidence for choice A—Aisha fought for <u>women's rights</u> to end <u>misogyny.</u>

Desolation

Find each of the following words on the *Twilight* page number provided. Based on the way each word is used in the book, guess at its definition.

1. **Plagued** (p. 145) might mean _____

   _____

2. **Threshold** (p. 145) might mean _____

   _____

3. **Desolation** (p. 145) might mean _____

   _____

4. **Shambled** (p. 145) might mean _____

   _____

5. **Compilation** (p. 147) might mean _____

   _____

6. **Tendrils** (p. 148) might mean _____

   _____

7. **Muddled** (p. 148) might mean _____

   _____

8. **Constructive** (p. 149) might mean _____

   _____

Let's see how you did. Check your answers, write the exact definitions,
and reread the sentence in *Twilight* where each word appears. Then
complete the drills.

1. **Plagued** (p. 145) means *deeply troubled*. It comes from the word
   plague, which refers to a *widespread disease.* The most famous
   plagues of all time: Moses' plague, the Black Death in 1346, the
   1855 Third Pandemic in China, and Bella's crush on Edward.

2. **Threshold** (p. 145) means *the floor of a doorway.*

3. **Desolation** (p. 145) means *total emptiness or misery.* Remember
   that *desolation* was a synonym for *despair* in Group 23. The other
   synonyms are: anguish, despondency, wretchedness.

4. **Shambled** (p. 145) means *moved with a slow, shuffling walk.* Here's
   another *walk* word, like *flit* and *lumber.* Remember that *flit* means
   to move quickly and lightly, like a bird. *Lumber* means *to move slowly
   and awkwardly,* like a zombie in a horror movie. Also, *veer* and
   wheel mean *to change direction suddenly.* All of these words can refer
   to the way you walk. A fancy term for the way you walk is *gait.*
   Standardized tests love to test the word *gait.* Horse lovers probably
   know this word already—it is also used to describe a horse's walk.

5. **Compilation** (p. 147) means *grouping,* like the mix of songs on
   your iPod, or the CD that Edward gave Bella. Oddly, *compilation*
   even looks like *com-* (with) and *pile—with a pile*—a grouping
   of items! This brings up the great SAT word *compendious* from
   Group 2. *Compendious* looks like *compilation,* so it makes sense that
   compendious should mean *comprehensive but concise.*

6. **Tendrils** (p. 148) can mean *strands of hair,* or *shoots of a climbing
   plant.*

7. **Muddled** (p. 148) means *confused.* It sounds a lot like *befuddled*
   from Group 15, which also means *confused.*

8. **Constructive** (p. 149) means *useful.*

Synonyms: Select the word or phrase whose meaning is closest to the word in capital letters.

1. PLAGUED
   A. bothered
   B. shambled
   C. compiled
   D. abhorred
   E. muddled

2. SHAMBLE
   A. wheel
   B. veer
   C. shuffle
   D. flit
   E. trot

3. MUDDLED
   A. despondent
   B. anguished
   C. befuddled
   D. immersed
   E. sodden

4. CONSTRUCTIVE
   A. proprietary
   B. combined
   C. slow
   D. confused
   E. useful

Analogies: Select the answer choice that best completes the meaning of the sentence.

5. Constructive is to superfluous as
   A. compilation is to compendious
   B. shambled is to lumbered
   C. desolate is to despondent
   D. indecisive is to resolute
   E. sedulous is to insolent

6. Plagued is to problem as
   A. muddled is to coherency
   B. jubilant is to victory
   C. anguished is to triumph
   D. euphoric is to disappointment
   E. tainted is to tendrils

Sentence Completions: Choose the word that, when inserted in the sentence, best fits the meaning of the sentence as a whole.

7. Even though it had been four weeks, Soiban was still _____ by Lorenzo's criticism of her painting; she could still hear it as though she had received it just yesterday.
   A. shambled
   B. muddled
   C. condemned
   D. plagued
   E. evaded

8. As soon as it crossed the threshold, Jimal was terrified both by the zombie's shambling _____ and by its desolate eyes.
   A. compilation
   B. opacity
   C. prudence
   D. abstraction
   E. gait

1. **A.** *Plagued* means *continually troubled*. Use the process of elimination; only choice A is close. *Shambled* means *shuffled slowly*, *abhorred* means *hated*, and *muddled* means *confused*.

2. **C.** *Shamble* means *shuffle*.

3. **C.** *Muddled* and *befuddled* mean *confused*. *Despondent* means *very sad and hopeless*, *anguished* means *suffering*, *immersed* means *submerged*, and *sodden* means *drenched*.

4. **E.** *Constructive* means *useful*. *Proprietary* means *possessive*.

5. **D.** "Constructive (useful) is the opposite of superfluous (unnecessary)."
    - A. Compilation (grouping) is the opposite of compendious (complete but concise) . . . no.
    - B. Shambled (shuffled) is the opposite of lumbered (walked heavily) . . . no, they are different, but not opposites.
    - C. Desolate (miserable) is the opposite of despondent (hopeless) . . . no.
    - (D.) Indecisive is the opposite of resolute (determined) . . . yes.
    - E. Sedulous (diligent) is the opposite of insolent (rude) . . . no, they are unrelated.

6. **B.** "Someone might feel plagued by a problem."
    - A. Someone might feel muddled (confused) by a coherency (clarity) . . . no.
    - (B.) Someone might feel jubilant (happy and triumphant) by a victory . . . yes!
    - C. Someone might feel anguished (miserable) by a triumph . . . no.
    - D. Someone might feel euphoric (thrilled) by a disappointment . . . no.
    - E. Someone might feel tainted (contaminated) by tendrils (strands of hair) . . . no.

7. **D.** "Even though it had been four weeks, Soiban was still *feeling criticized* by Lorenzo's criticism of her painting; she could still hear it as though she had received it just yesterday."
    Plagued means *deeply troubled* and is the best answer. *Condemned* means *disapproved of* or *found guilty* and does not work quite as well as *plagued*, since the last part of the sentence, "she could still hear it," indicates that the criticism still troubles her.

8. **E.** "As soon as it crossed the threshold, Jimal was terrified both by the zombie's shambling *walk* and by its desolate eyes."
    Gait means *style of walk*, like a horse's gait. *Opacity* is *solidness*, *prudence* is *wisdom*, and *abstraction* is *an idea*.

Solutions

I. Let's review some of the words that you've seen in Groups 21–25. Match each of the following words to the correct definition or synonym on the right. Then check the solutions on page 172.

1. Amity		A.	Inferior
2. Substandard		B.	Feasible
3. Abhor		C.	Dubious
4. Plausible		D.	Nefarious
5. Fidelity		E.	Assiduous
6. Cadence		F.	Vacillating
7. Incredulous		G.	Despondent
8. Pernicious		H.	Loyalty
9. Serene		I.	Friendship
10. Industrious		J.	Engrossed
11. Immersed		K.	Rhythm
12. Irresolute		L.	Placid
13. Desolate		M.	Hate
14. Compilation		N.	Confused
15. Muddled		O.	Grouping

II. Let's review several of the word parts that you've seen in Groups 21–25. Match each of the following word parts to the correct definition or synonym on the right. Then check the solutions on page 172.

16. Sub-		A.	Through or across
17. In-, Im-		B.	Believe
18. Mort-		C.	Under or below
19. Cred-		D.	Hate
20. Trans-		E.	Not
21. Mis-		F.	Death

Raucous Run-In

Find each of the following words on the *Twilight* page number provided. Based on the way each word is used in the book, guess at its definition.

1. **Exponentially** (p. 151) might mean _____

   _____

2. **Estrogen** (p. 152) might mean _____

   _____

3. **Picturesque** (p. 153) might mean _____

   _____

4. **Nonchalant** (p. 155) might mean _____

   _____

5. **Raucously** (p. 157) might mean _____

   _____

6. **Automatically** (p. 157) might mean _____

   _____

7. **Chortling** (p. 158) might mean _____

   _____

8. **Incapacitate** (p. 161) might mean _____

   _____

Let's see how you did. Check your answers, write the exact definitions, and reread the sentence in *Twilight* where each word appears. Then complete the drills.

Definitions

1. **Exponentially** (p. 151) means *more and more rapidly.* This word comes from the math concept that as the value of an exponent increases, the result increases more and more rapidly. For example, $3^2 = 9$, but $3^5 = 243$. Okay, that's the only math in this whole book, I promise!

2. **Estrogen** (p. 152) literally refers to *female hormones,* but it can also be used informally to refer to *female bonding.*

3. **Picturesque** (p. 153) means *quaint and pretty.* Remember *statuesque,* from Group 4, meaning *attractively tall and imposing*—like a statue of a Greek goddess? It turns out that *-esque* means *resembling,* so *statuesque* means *resembling a statue,* and *picturesque* means *resembling a picture,* like a postcard!

4. **Nonchalant** (p. 155) means *casual and calm* or *uninterested.* Synonyms: dispassionate, indifferent.

5. **Raucously** (p. 157) means *loudly and harshly.* This word reminds me of the word *blaring* from Group 21. Awesome related words for *raucous:* clamorous (loudly protesting), obstreperous (noisy and unruly), strident (making a loud grating noise), vociferous (loudly shouting).

6. **Automatically** (p. 157) means *happening by itself—without conscious intention.* The prefix *auto-* means *self,* like *autobiography* (self-told life story), *automobile* (self-moving vehicle), and *autonomous* (self-ruling—independent).

7. **Chortling** (p. 158) basically means *chuckling.* This word was actually invented by Lewis Carroll in the stories of *Alice in Wonderland.* It's a mixture of the words *chuckle* and *snort!*

8. **Incapacitate** (p. 161) means *paralyze.* Synonym: debilitate.

Synonyms: Select the word or phrase whose meaning is closest to the word in capital letters.

1. PICTURESQUE
   A. rapid
   B. casual
   C. scenic
   D. automatic
   E. humorous

2. NONCHALANT
   A. exponential
   B. raucous
   C. obstreperous
   D. vociferous
   E. dispassionate

3. DEBILITATE
   A. sprawl
   B. incapacitate
   C. blare
   D. plague
   E. shamble

4. CLAMOROUS
   A. chortling
   B. muddled
   C. raucous
   D. desolate
   E. anguished

Analogies: Select the answer choice that best completes the meaning of the sentence.

5. Chortling is to hysterical as
   A. apathetic is to nonchalant
   B. dislike is to loathe
   C. automatic is to autonomous
   D. obstreperous is to vociferous
   E. gynecologist is to estrogen

6. Solitary is to autonomous as
   A. reclusive is to chaotic
   B. transparent is to anarchistic
   C. communal is to group-oriented
   D. remorseful is to penitent
   E. contrite is to repentant

Sentence Completions: Choose the word that, when inserted in the sentence, best fits the meaning of the sentence as a whole.

7. After the author appeared on *Oprah,* sales of her book increased _____; the book even became a bestseller for the week.
   A. nonchalantly
   B. autobiographically
   C. exponentially
   D. raucously
   E. constructively

8. The mayor was worried about the effect of the lively music festival and hoped that _____ crowds would not taint the picturesque mountain town.
   A. obstreperous
   B. automatic
   C. chortling
   D. industrious
   E. immersed

Solutions

1. **C.** *Picturesque* means *quaint and pretty,* like a postcard, so *scenic* is the best answer. *Automatic* means *involuntary.*

2. **E.** *Nonchalant* means *casual or uninterested.* That's also what *dispassionate* means. This is an interesting word to break apart. Since *dis-* means *not, dispassionate* means *not passionate*—*casual or uninterested. Exponential* means *more and more rapidly. Raucous, obstreperous,* and *vociferous* mean loud in slightly different ways.

3. **B.** *Debilitate* and *incapacitate* mean *prevent from functioning.*

4. **C.** *Clamorous* means *loudly protesting. Raucous,* which means *loud and harsh,* is the closest answer. As always, use the process of elimination to find the closest answer—cross off answers that you are sure don't work and choose the best of what's left. *Chortling* means *chuckling,* and *muddled* means *confused. Desolate* and *anguished* mean *miserable.*

5. **B.** "Chortling (chuckling) is a smaller version of hysterical (uncontrolled emotion)."
    A. Apathetic is a smaller version of nonchalant . . . no, they both mean *uninterested.*
    (B.) Dislike is a smaller version of loathing (hating) . . . yes.
    C. Automatic (reflexive) is a smaller version of autonomous (independent) . . . no.
    D. Obstreperous is a smaller version of vociferous . . . no, they both mean *noisy.*
    E. Gynecologist is a smaller version of estrogen . . . no, but a *gynecologist* is *a doctor who specializes in female health,* so she or he certainly knows about estrogen.

6. **C.** "A solitary (alone) person is autonomous (independent)."
    A. A reclusive (solitary) person is chaotic (disorganized) . . . no.
    B. A transparent (see-through) person is anarchistic (anti-government) . . . no.
    (C.) A communal person is group-oriented . . . yes.
    D. A remorseful person is penitent . . . no, they both mean *regretful.*
    E. A contrite person is repentant . . . no, they both mean *regretful.*

7. **C.** "After the author appeared on *Oprah,* sales of her book increased *lots;* the book even became a bestseller for the week."
    Exponentially means *more and more rapidly.* Choice A, *autobiographically* (self-written) is about books, but not about sales increasing. Choice E, *constructively* (helpfully), does not fit.

8. **A.** "The mayor was worried about the effect of the lively music festival and hoped that *lively* crowds would not taint the picturesque mountain town."
    Obstreperous, meaning *noisy and difficult to control,* fits best. *Industrious* (diligent) or *immersed* (engrossed) crowds would not "taint" the town.

A Dazzling Rescuer

Find each of the following words on the *Twilight* page number provided. Based on the way each word is used in the book, guess at its definition.

1. **Fishtailed** (p. 162) might mean _____

   _____

2. **Curtly** (p. 163) might mean _____

   _____

3. **Vague** (p. 163) might mean _____

   _____

4. **Make amends** (p. 163) might mean _____

   _____

5. **Scrutinize** (p. 166) might mean _____

   _____

6. **Obstinate** (p. 166) might mean _____

   _____

7. **Dazzle** (p. 167) might mean _____

   _____

8. **Repressing** (p. 169) might mean _____

   _____

Let's see how you did. Check your answers, write the exact definitions, and reread the sentence in *Twilight* where each word appears. Then complete the drills.

1. **Fishtailed** (p. 162) means *the back moved sideways,* like a fish's tail when swimming, and like cars rounding corners in *Fast and Furious.*

2. **Curtly** (p. 163) means *in a brief and sharp way.* Synonyms for *curt:* abrupt, brusque, gruff (grouchy), laconic, surly (hostile), terse (brief, but less rude).

3. **Vague** (p. 163) means *unclear* or *indefinite.* Synonyms: ambiguous, amorphous. *Amorphous* is a wonderful word to break apart. *A-* means *without,* as in *amoral* and *atypical,* and *morph-* refers to *shape.* So *amorphous* means *without clear shape—vague.*

4. **Make amends** (p. 163) means *make up for* or *compensate.* This reminds me of the word *amend,* from Group 12, which means *added to correct or improve.* You can see the connection. To make amends is to correct a situation by making up for something. Synonyms: atone, expiate, indemnify (compensate for harm or loss), redress.

5. **Scrutinize** (p. 166) means *closely examine.*

6. **Obstinate** (p. 166) means *stubborn.* If you are a *Twilight* fan and know Bella and Edward pretty well, then this word is easy to remember because both of them are incredibly stubborn! Synonyms: intractable, obdurate, pertinacious (stubborn and annoying), recalcitrant (stubbornly uncooperative with authority), tenacious.

7. **Dazzle** (p. 167) means *stun with charm, skills, or appeal.* Vampires dazzle their victims, and Edward dazzles Bella quite often . . .

8. **Repressing** (p. 169) means *suppressing.* Remember *suppress* from Group 8? These two words mean exactly what they sound like—*pressing things down.*

Synonyms: Select the word or phrase whose meaning is closest to the word in capital letters.

1. LACONIC
   A. fishtail
   B. curt
   C. vague
   D. ambiguous
   E. amorphous

2. ATONE
   A. expiate
   B. brusque
   C. terse
   D. scrutinize
   E. charm

3. OBSTINATE
   A. nonchalant
   B. indifferent
   C. dispassionate
   D. apathetic
   E. obdurate

4. DAZZLING
   A. repressive
   B. vague
   C. exponential
   D. overwhelming
   E. clamorous

Analogies: Select the answer choice that best completes the meaning of the sentence.

5. Curt is to verbose as
   A. laconic is to gruff
   B. alluring is to heinous
   C. terse is to prattling
   D. plausible is to feasible
   E. encroaching is to intruding

6. Scrutinize is to glance at as
   A. repress is to suppress
   B. fishtail is to wheel
   C. curt is to abrupt
   D. alluring is to repellant
   E. recalcitrant is to pertinacious

Sentence Completions: Choose the word that, when inserted in the sentence, <u>best</u> fits the meaning of the sentence as a whole.

7. Eighth-grade girls could not resist Evan's _____; they attended all his wrestling matches and facebooked him incessantly.
   A. diplomacy
   B. haste
   C. allure
   D. reproach
   E. prudence

8. Gabe's blue bike _____ while he skidded to avoid the marsh that encroached the trail.
   A. scrawled
   B. animated
   C. disheveled
   D. fishtailed
   E. lumbered

1. **B.** *Laconic* and *curt* mean *brief. Vague, ambiguous,* and *amorphous* mean *unclear* or *indistinct.*

2. **A.** *Atone* and *expiate* mean *make up for. Brusque* and *terse* mean *short and rude. Scrutinize* means *examine closely.*

3. **E.** *Obstinate* and *obdurate* mean *stubborn. Nonchalant, dispassionate,* and *apathetic* mean *casual and indifferent. Apathetic* is a terrific word to break apart. *A-* means *without,* and *path-* refers to *feeling,* so *apathetic* means *without feeling.*

4. **D.** *Dazzling* means *stunning. Repressive* means *restraining, vague* means *unclear, exponential* means *more and more rapid,* and *clamorous* means *noisy.*

5. **C.** "Curt (brief) is the opposite of verbose (wordy)."
   A. Laconic (brief) is the opposite of gruff (grumpy) . . . no.
   B. Alluring (charming) is the opposite of heinous (shockingly evil) . . . no.
   C. Terse (brief) is the opposite of prattling (babbling) . . . yes, Angela is the opposite of Jessica!
   D. Plausible (believable) is the opposite of feasible (possible) . . . no.
   E. Encroaching (intruding) is the opposite of intruding . . . no.

6. **D.** "Scrutinize (examine closely) is the opposite of glance at."
   A. Repress is the opposite of suppress . . . no, they both mean *restrain.*
   B. Fishtail is the opposite of wheel . . . no, they are different movements, but not opposites.
   C. Curt is the opposite of abrupt . . . no, they both mean *brief.*
   D. Alluring (appealing) is the opposite of repellant (disgusting) . . . yes.
   E. Recalcitrant is the opposite of pertinacious . . . no, both mean *stubborn.*

7. **C.** "Eighth-grade girls could not resist Evan's <u>*appeal;*</u> they attended all his wrestling matches and facebooked him incessantly."
   Allure means *appeal. Diplomacy* means *tactfulness, haste* means *hurriedness, reproach* means *scolding,* and *prudence* means *wisdom.*

8. **D.** "Gabe's blue bike <u>*skidded*</u> while he skidded to avoid the marsh that encroached the trail."
   Fishtailed means *the back moved sideways,* which could happen during a skid. That is certainly the best answer using the process of elimination. *Scrawled* means *wrote messily, animated* means *lively, disheveled* means *messy,* and *lumbered* means *walked awkwardly.*

Convoluted Theories

Find each of the following words on the *Twilight* page number provided. Based on the way each word is used in the book, guess at its definition.

1. **Coy** (p. 169) might mean _____

_____

2. **Alabaster** (p. 170) might mean _____

_____

3. **Furrowed** (p. 170) might mean _____

_____

4. **Indifferent** (p. 171) might mean _____

_____

5. **Convoluted** (p. 173) might mean _____

_____

6. **Hypothetically** (p. 173) might mean _____

_____

7. **Curb** (p. 173) might mean _____

_____

8. **Unequivocally** (p. 174) might mean _____

_____

Let's see how you did. Check your answers, write the exact definitions, and reread the sentence in *Twilight* where each word appears. Then complete the drills.

1. **Coy** (p. 169) means *intentionally (or even manipulatively) cute, warm, and attentive*. *Gossip Girl*'s Serena is serene, and I'd say that Blair Waldorf can be pretty coy, especially towards Nate, Chuck, and even her dad.

2. **Alabaster** (p. 170) is *a translucent, white mineral*. I remember this word because it sounds like plaster, which is usually white.

3. **Furrowed** (p. 170) means *wrinkled from frowning*.

4. **Indifferent** (p. 171) means *unconcerned*. This was a synonym for *nonchalant* in Group 26. The other synonym was *dispassionate*. You also learned *apathetic* in the drills and solutions of Group 27. All of these words imply *not caring*.

5. **Convoluted** (p. 173) means *complicated and difficult to follow*. This word is the opposite of *coherent,* from Group 14. Synonyms: byzantine, elaborate. Congratulations, you've just joined the twelve people on the planet who know the word *byzantine*. But that's a good thing, because I've actually seen this word on the SAT!

6. **Hypothetically** (p. 173) means *in theory,* it even looks like the word *theoretically*.

7. **Curb** (p. 173) means *restrain*. So, the title of the HBO series *Curb Your Enthusiasm* means *restrain your enthusiasm*.

8. **Unequivocally** (p. 174) means *definitely*. Synonyms: indubitably, unambiguously. Both of these synonyms are formed from words that you've seen already. *Unambiguously* means *not ambiguous* or *not unclear*. And *indubitably* means *not dubious* or *not doubtable*.

Synonyms: Select the word or phrase whose meaning is closest to the word in capital letters.

1. ALABASTER
   A. white
   B. ocher
   C. russet
   D. auburn
   E. burgundy

2. INDIFFERENT
   A. sympathetic
   B. empathetic
   C. apathetic
   D. pathetic
   E. fervent

3. CONVOLUTED
   A. coy
   B. hypothetical
   C. byzantine
   D. furrowed
   E. unequivocal

4. UNAMBIGUOUSLY
   A. coherently
   B. vehemently
   C. ominously
   D. audaciously
   E. indubitably

Analogies: Select the answer choice that best completes the meaning of the sentence.

5. Curb is to repressing as
   A. vague is to vivid
   B. verbose is to laconic
   C. droning is to animated
   D. intractable is to recalcitrant
   E. redress is to offensive

6. Maze is to convoluted as
   A. russet is to alabaster
   B. vagueness is to unequivocal
   C. brow is to furrowed
   D. library is to obstreperous
   E. construct is to blaring

Sentence Completions: Choose the word that, when inserted in the sentence, best fits the meaning of the sentence as a whole.

7. Wilson furrowed his brow at the _____ logic of his lab mates and suggested that they rewrite their incoherent lab reports.
   A. indifferent
   B. apathetic
   C. convoluted
   D. coy
   E. alluring

8. Some books are so complex and involve such _____ plot twists that one needs to reread them several times.
   A. unequivocal
   B. byzantine
   C. hypothetical
   D. nefarious
   E. heinous

Solutions

1. **A.** *Alabaster* means *translucent white,* so choice A is best. *Ocher* means *brownish-yellow, russet* means *reddish-brown, auburn* means *reddish-brown* (usually for hair), and *burgundy* means *deep red.*

2. **C.** *Indifferent* means *uncaring.* That's also what *apathetic* means. *Sympathetic* means *feeling compassion for someone, empathetic* means *feeling with someone—sharing their emotions* (like Peter in *Heroes*), *pathetic* means *pitiful,* and *fervent* means *passionate.*

3. **C.** *Convoluted* and *byzantine* mean *complicated. Coy* means *cute (in a negative way), hypothetical* means *theoretical, furrowed* means *creased,* and *unequivocal* means *definite.*

4. **E.** *Unambiguously* and *indubitably* mean *undoubtedly. Coherently* means *logically, vehemently* means *with passion, ominously* means *threateningly,* and *audaciously* means *boldly.*

5. **D.** "Curb means repressing."
   A. Vague means vivid . . . no, *vague* means *unclear,* and *vivid* means *very clear.*
   B. Verbose (wordy) means laconic (brief) . . . no, they are opposites.
   C. Droning (repeating) means animated (lively) . . . no, they are opposites.
   (D.) Intractable means recalcitrant . . . yes, they both mean *stubborn.*
   E. Redress (make amends) means offensive . . . no, they are almost opposites.

6. **C.** "A maze can be convoluted (complex)."
   A. A russet (reddish-brown) can be alabaster (translucent white) . . . no.
   B. A vagueness (unclearness) can be unequivocal (certain) . . . no.
   (C.) A brow can be furrowed (creased from concentration) . . . yes.
   D. A library can be obstreperous (noisy and unruly) . . . no, not if my high school librarian has anything to say about it.
   E. A construct (theory) can be blaring (noisy) . . . no, that makes no sense.

7. **C.** "Wilson furrowed his brow at the _incoherent_ logic of his lab mates and suggested that they rewrite their incoherent lab reports."
   Convoluted means *complicated and difficult to follow.* That's pretty close to what *incoherent* means.

8. **B.** "Some books are so complex and involve such _complex_ plot twists that one needs to reread them several times."
   Byzantine means *complex.* Several other answers sound decent when placed in the blank, but only *byzantine* is supported by the evidence in the question. The sentence tells you that the blank relates to complexity, not to a theory (*hypothetical*) or to wickedness (*nefarious* and *heinous*).

Enigmatic Answers

Find each of the following words on the *Twilight* page number provided. Based on the way each word is used in the book, guess at its definition.

1. **Fervent** (p. 174) might mean _____

   _____

2. **Catastrophes** (p. 174) might mean _____

   _____

3. **Grave** (p. 175) might mean _____

   _____

4. **Evasiveness** (p. 179) might mean _____

   _____

5. **Enigmatic** (p. 180) might mean _____

   _____

6. **Modulate** (p. 182) might mean _____

   _____

7. **Abide by** (p. 182) might mean _____

   _____

8. **Bleak** (p. 184) might mean _____

   _____

Let's see how you did. Check your answers, write the exact definitions, and reread the sentence in *Twilight* where each word appears. Then complete the drills.

1. **Fervent** (p. 174) means *passionate*. You saw this word as a synonym for *vehement* in Group 11. The other synonym was *fervid*. More synonyms: ardent, avid, keen, zealous.

2. **Catastrophes** (p. 174) means *disasters*.

3. **Grave** (p. 175) means *serious* or *solemn*. It is related to the word *gravity*, which can mean *serious or heavy*—the same word for the force that keeps your feet on the ground.

4. **Evasiveness** (p. 179) means *avoidance*, just like *evade*, from Group 7, means *avoid*. You learned the following great synonyms for *evade*: circumvent, elude, equivocate, prevaricate.

5. **Enigmatic** (p. 180) means *mysterious*. *Enigmatic* was a synonym for *cryptic* in Group 16. The other synonyms for cryptic were *abstruse, ambiguous, arcane, oracular,* and *recondite*. *Enigmatic* reminds me of a great *Seinfeld* scene. Jerry is upset to learn that Newman previously dated his girlfriend. Elaine suggests that maybe there's more to Newman than they know, saying, "He's an **enigma**, a mystery wrapped in a riddle." Jerry, never too fond of Newman, responds "Yeah, he's a mystery wrapped in a Twinkie." (NBC, *Seinfeld,* "The Big Salad," 1994)

6. **Modulate** (p. 182) means *regulate* or *change the tone of.*

7. **Abide by** (p. 182) means *obey*.

8. **Bleak** (p. 184) in this case means *cold and forbidding*—Edward is afraid to let Bella in, afraid for her safety. To determine the meaning of a word in context, look at the words and sentences around it. A few sentences earlier, Edward calls himself a monster, and then a few sentences later he says that Bella's insane for not being concerned that's he's a vampire. He is terrified of hurting her, actually biting her, to be specific.

Synonyms: Select the word or phrase whose meaning is closest to the word in capital letters.

1. FERVENT
   A. grave
   B. evasive
   C. keen
   D. modulated
   E. bleak

2. CATASTROPHE
   A. disaster
   B. gravity
   C. nonchalance
   D. clamor
   E. chortle

3. SOLEMN
   A. enigmatic
   B. modulated
   C. coy
   D. elaborate
   E. grave

4. ENIGMATIC
   A. apathetic
   B. curbed
   C. unequivocal
   D. ambiguous
   E. zealous

Analogies: Select the answer choice that best completes the meaning of the sentence.

5. Fervent is to apathetic as
   A. ardent is to indifferent
   B. grave is to bleak
   C. dispassionate is to nonchalant
   D. vogue is to stylish
   E. indubitably is to unequivocally

6. Catastrophe is to somber as
   A. compilation is to muddled
   B. scrutiny is to incredulous
   C. immersion is to indecisive
   D. threshold is to desolate
   E. plague is to apprehensive

Sentence Completions: Choose the word that, when inserted in the sentence, <u>best</u> fits the meaning of the sentence as a whole.

7. The students abided by all the rules in the library and _____ their voices so other students could study.
   A. observed
   B. concealed
   C. vacillated
   D. modulated
   E. tainted

8. The commission warned that an environmental catastrophe would have _____ effects.
   A. evasive
   B. raucous
   C. vociferous
   D. proprietary
   E. grave

1. **C.** *Fervent* and *keen* mean *passionate*. *Keen* can also mean *sharp* or *penetrating*. *Grave* means *serious, evasive* means *avoiding, modulated* means *regulated,* and *bleak* means *forbidding*.

2. **A.** *Catastrophe* means *disaster*. *Nonchalance* means *casualness, clamor* means *noise,* and *chortle* means *chuckle*.

3. **E.** *Solemn* and *grave* mean *serious*. *Enigmatic* means *mysterious, coy* means *cute,* and *elaborate* means *detailed or complex*.

4. **D.** *Enigmatic* means *mysterious,* so *ambiguous,* which means *unclear* or *inexact,* is the best answer. Use the process of elimination. *Apathetic* means *indifferent,* *curbed* means *restrained, unequivocal* means *definite,* and *zealous* means *passionate*. It makes sense that *ambiguous* means *inexact; ambi-* means *both ways,* so *ambiguous* means *going both ways—unsure*.

5. **A.** "Fervent (passionate) is the opposite of apathetic (indifferent)."
   - (A.) Ardent (passionate) is the opposite of indifferent . . . yes.
   - B . Grave (serious) is the opposite of bleak (forbidding) . . . no, they are similar.
   - C . Dispassionate (rational) is the opposite of nonchalant (casual) . . . no, they are similar.
   - D. Vogue (stylish) is the opposite of stylish . . . no.
   - E . Indubitably (definitely) is the opposite of unequivocally (definitely) . . . no.

6. **E.** "A catastrophe would probably make people somber (gloomy)."
   - A . A compilation (gathering) would probably make people muddled (confused) . . . no.
   - B . A scrutiny (close examination) would probably make people incredulous (doubtful) . . . no.
   - C . An immersion (submersion) would probably make people indecisive . . . no.
   - D. A threshold (entryway) would probably make people desolate (unhappy) . . . no.
   - (E.) A plague (widespread disease) would probably make people apprehensive (worried) . . . yes.

7. **D.** "The students abided by all the rules in the library and <u>lowered</u> their voices so other students could study."

   Modulated means *regulated,* and is the best answer. *Observed, concealed* (hid), and *vacillated* (wavered) almost work, but *modulated* relates better to voice and the flow of the sentence.

8. **E.** "The commission warned that an environmental catastrophe would have <u>bad/catastrophic</u> effects."

   Grave means *serious*. *Evasive* means *avoiding, raucous* means *noisy, vociferous* means *noisy shouting,* and *proprietary* means *pertaining to ownership*.

Group 30

Unconditional Agreement

Find each of the following words on the *Twilight* page number provided. Based on the way each word is used in the book, guess at its definition.

1. **Complacent** (p. 187) might mean _____
   _____

2. **Recoiled** (p. 187) might mean _____
   _____

3. **Unscathed** (p. 189) might mean _____
   _____

4. **Ruefully** (p. 189) might mean _____
   _____

5. **Anguished** (p. 190) might mean _____
   _____

6. **Appalled** (p. 190) might mean _____
   _____

7. **Unconditional** (p. 192) might mean _____
   _____

8. **Mechanically** (p. 193) might mean _____
   _____

Let's see how you did. Check your answers, write the exact definitions, and reread the sentence in *Twilight* where each word appears. Then complete the drills.

Definitions

1. **Complacent** (p. 187) means *smug and self-satisfied*. This word is often used to indicate that one is too at ease and therefore unaware of actual danger, such as the danger of dating a vampire.

2. **Recoiled** (p. 187) means *flinched back*. This word means exactly what it sounds like. Imagine a snake that's coiled up and comes forward, but then recoils—it backs away and winds itself back up. *Re-* means *again*, as in reborn, reclaim, reapply, and resend.

3. **Unscathed** (p. 189) means *unharmed*. I remember this word's meaning because *scathe* sounds like *scar*, so *unscathed* sounds like *unscarred*.

4. **Ruefully** (p. 189) means *regretfully*. *Family Guy*'s Stewie has been known to say, "You shall rue this day!" (Fox, *Family Guy*, "Mind Over Murder," 1999)

5. **Anguished** (p. 190) means *pained*. *Anguish* was a synonym for *despair* in Group 23. The other synonyms were *desolation, despondency,* and *wretchedness.*

6. **Appalled** (p. 190) means *greatly distressed*. This word actually comes from the word *pale,* as in losing color in your face when unexpectantly meeting vampires on the baseball field.

7. **Unconditional** (p. 192) means *total* or *subject to no conditions*. Synonyms: absolute, categorical, unequivocal (from Group 28, meaning *definite*), unmitigated, unqualified, untempered. Remember, you learned in Group 16 that *qualified* means *with reservation* or *to make less complete,* so *unqualified* means *without reservation—subject to no conditions.* A great synonym for *qualify* is *temper.* The SAT, ACT, and SSAT love to use these words!

8. **Mechanically** (p. 193) means *automatically* or *without thinking,* like a machine.

Synonyms: Select the word or phrase whose meaning is closest to the word in capital letters.

1. COMPLACENT
   - A. smug
   - B. recoiled
   - C. unscathed
   - D. anguished
   - E. despondent

2. RUEFUL
   - A. qualified
   - B. mechanical
   - C. regretful
   - D. complimentary
   - E. animated

3. UNCONDITIONAL
   - A. saturated
   - B. sodden
   - C. disheveled
   - D. inexplicable
   - E. absolute

4. TEMPER
   - A. elude
   - B. prevaricate
   - C. equivocate
   - D. moderate
   - E. lumber

Analogies: Select the answer choice that best completes the meaning of the sentence.

5. Unconditional is to qualified as
   - A. complacent is to self-satisfied
   - B. recoiled is to anguished
   - C. broached is to mechanical
   - D. unmitigated is to attenuated
   - E. appalled is to pallid

6. Unscathed is to catastrophe as
   - A. pallid is to alabaster
   - B. placid is to censure
   - C. scrutinized is to furrowing
   - D. recalcitrant is to exam
   - E. enigmatic is to downpour

Sentence Completions: Choose the word or words that, when inserted in the sentence, <u>best</u> fits the meaning of the sentence as a whole.

7. Rose _____ recoiled after she accidentally rested her hand on the hot stove; the speed of her response left her hand _____ and totally free of burns.
   - A. automatically .. anguished
   - B. appallingly .. mechanical
   - C. fervently .. modulated
   - D. gravely .. furrowed
   - E. mechanically .. unscathed

8. Sitting in detention, Sam remembered _____ the events of the day that had landed him there, and was appalled at his behavior.
   - A. ruefully
   - B. unconditionally
   - C. complacently
   - D. indifferently
   - E. obstinately

1. **A.** *Complacent* means *smug. Recoiled* means *flinched back, unscathed* means *unharmed, anguished* means *pained,* and *despondent* means *miserable.*

2. **C.** *Rueful* means *regretful. Qualified* means *limited, mechanical* means *automatic, complimentary* means *praising,* and *animated* means *energetic.*

3. **E.** *Unconditional* and *absolute* mean *complete. Saturated* and *sodden* mean *soaked, disheveled* means *messy,* and *inexplicable* means *unexplainable.*

4. **D.** *Temper* can mean *lessen.* That's also what *moderate* means. Use the process of elimination. *Elude, prevaricate,* and *equivocate* all mean *avoid. Lumber* means *walk awkwardly.*

5. **D.** "Unconditional (without conditions) is the opposite of qualified (with conditions)."
   A. Complacent is the opposite of self-satisfied . . . no, they are synonyms.
   B. Recoiled (flinched back) is the opposite of anguished (pained) . . . no.
   C. Broached (brought up) is the opposite of mechanical (automatic) . . . no, they are unrelated.
   (D.) Unmitigated (unqualified) is the opposite of attenuated (reduced) . . . yes, this is the best of the answer choices.
   E. Appalled (distressed) is the opposite of pallid (pale) . . . no.

6. **B.** "She is fortunate to be unscathed after a catastrophe."
   A. She is fortunate to be pallid (pale) after an alabaster (white) . . . no, that makes no sense.
   (B.) She is fortunate to be placid (peaceful) after a censure (harsh criticism) . . . yes.
   C. She is fortunate to be scrutinized (closely examined) after a furrowing (wrinkling) . . . no.
   D. She is fortunate to be recalcitrant (stubborn) after an exam . . . no, that makes no sense.
   E. She is fortunate to be enigmatic (mysterious) after a downpour . . . no.

7. **E.** "Rose _quickly_ recoiled after she accidentally rested her hand on the hot stove; the speed of her response left her hand _unharmed_ and totally free of burns."
   Use the process of elimination, one blank at a time. Choice E is best. *Mechanically* means *automatically* (like a reflex), and *unscathed* means *unharmed.*

8. **A.** "Sitting in detention, Sam remembered _regretfully_ the events of the day that had landed him there, and was appalled at his behavior."
   Ruefully means *regretfully.*

Quiz 6

I. Let's review some of the words that you've seen in Groups 26–30. Match each of the following words to the correct definition or synonym on the right. Then check the solutions on page 172.

1. Picturesque	A. Debilitate
2. Obstreperous	B. Examine closely
3. Incapacitate	C. Apathetic
4. Curt	D. Noisy
5. Scrutinize	E. Quaint
6. Obdurate	F. Indubitably
7. Indifferent	G. Laconic
8. Byzantine	H. Ardent
9. Unequivocally	I. Obstinate
10. Fervent	J. Regretful
11. Catastrophic	K. Complex
12. Modulate	L. Greatly distressed
13. Rueful	M. Unqualified
14. Appalled	N. Regulate
15. Unconditional	O. Disastrous

II. Let's review several of the word parts that you've seen in Groups 26–30. Match each of the following word parts to the correct definition or synonym on the right. Then check the solutions on page 172.

16. -Esque	A. Self
17. Auto-	B. Without
18. -Morph	C. Resembling
19. A-	D. Again
20. Re-	E. Not
21. In-	F. Shape

Group 31

Conspicuous Indulgence

Find each of the following words on the *Twilight* page number provided. Based on the way each word is used in the book, guess at its definition.

1. **Vain** (p. 197) might mean _____

   _____

2. **Colossal** (p. 197) might mean _____

   _____

3. **Shrouded** (p. 198) might mean _____

   _____

4. **Candid** (p. 198) might mean _____

   _____

5. **Belatedly** (p. 198) might mean _____

   _____

6. **Ostentatious** (p. 199) might mean _____

   _____

7. **Conspicuous** (p. 199) might mean _____

   _____

8. **Indulgence** (p. 199) might mean _____

   _____

Let's see how you did. Check your answers, write the exact definitions,
and reread the sentence in *Twilight* where each word appears. Then
complete the drills.

1. **Vain** (p. 197) in this case means *useless*. It can also mean *conceited*.
   Synonym: futile.

2. **Colossal** (p. 197) means *huge*, like the Roman Coliseum, which
   could seat over 80,000 spectators. To me, this word sounds
   huge—my voice even deepens when I say it.

3. **Shrouded** (p. 198) means *covered*. It was a synonym for *veiled* in
   Group 10. *Shroud* actually comes from the name of the cloth, a
   shroud, used to **cover** a dead person for burial.

4. **Candid** (p. 198) means *upfront and truthful*. That's where the name
   for *Candid Camera* (the precursor for all reality TV shows, such as
   American Idol, The Hills, and *America's Next Top Model*) came from.
   Candid Camera filmed real situations, not scripted ones. Synonyms:
   blunt, frank, sincere.

5. **Belatedly** (p. 198) means *later than it should have*. It just comes
   from the words *be late*.

6. **Ostentatious** (p. 199) means *over the top display of wealth*.
   Synonyms: pretentious, showy.

7. **Conspicuous** (p. 199) means *clearly visible* or *standing out*. This is
   a cool word to break apart. *Con-* means *with*, and *spic-*, like *spec-*,
   pertains to *vision* (spectacles). So, *conspicuous* means *with vision—
   clearly visible*. Synonyms: blatant, patent.

8. **Indulgence** (p. 199) means *a pleasure that one allows oneself.*

Synonyms: Select the word or phrase whose meaning is closest to the word in capital letters.

1. VAIN
    A. conspicuous
    B. belated
    C. shrouded
    D. futile
    E. frank

2. COLOSSAL
    A. huge
    B. ostentatious
    C. complacent
    D. rueful
    E. assuaged

3. CANDID
    A. appalled
    B. blunt
    C. unscathed
    D. unmitigated
    E. fervent

4. OSTENTATIOUS
    A. zealous
    B. enigmatic
    C. bleak
    D. unequivocal
    E. pretentious

Analogies: Select the answer choice that best completes the meaning of the sentence.

5. Shroud is to broach as
    A. surreptitious is to conspicuous
    B. indulgent is to decadent
    C. blatant is to patent
    D. belated is to candid
    E. cover is to veil

6. Candid is to furtive as
    A. vain is to futile
    B. colossal is to infinitesimal
    C. ostentatious is to showy
    D. recoil is to repress
    E. rue is to atone

Sentence Completions: Choose the word or words that, when inserted in the sentence, best fits the meaning of the sentence as a whole.

7. Fog _____ the runway, and the passengers anticipated an imminent announcement from the captain postponing takeoff.
    A. shrouded
    B. belated
    C. indulged
    D. fishtailed
    E. modulated

8. Plans to move the _____ statue of Nero proved _____; it was simply too large to transport.
    A. conspicuous .. belated
    B. colossal .. futile
    C. complacent .. unscathed
    D. indifferent .. automatic
    E. mechanical .. constructive

1. **D.** *Vain* and *futile* mean *useless. Conspicuous* means *obvious, belated*
means *late, shrouded* means *covered,* and *frank* means *direct.*
2. **A.** *Colossal* means *huge,* like the Roman Coliseum. *Ostentatious* means *showy, complacent* means *smug, rueful* means *regretful,* and *assuaged* means *soothed.*
3. **B.** *Candid* means *blunt,* like a reality TV show. *Appalled* means *distressed, unscathed* means *unharmed, unmitigated* means *absolute,* and *fervent* means *vehement.*
4. **E.** *Ostentatious* and *pretentious* mean *showy. Zealous* means *passionate, enigmatic* means *mysterious, bleak* means *forbidding,* and *unequivocal* means *definite.*
5. **A.** "Shroud (cover) is the opposite of broach (bring up)."
   - A. Surreptitious (secretive) is the opposite of conspicuous (obvious) . . . yes.
   - B. Indulgent (pleasure-seeking) is the opposite of decadent (self-indulgent) . . . no.
   - C. Blatant (obvious) is the opposite of patent (obvious) . . . no, they are synonyms.
   - D. Belated (late) is the opposite of candid (frank) . . . no, they are unrelated.
   - E. Cover is the opposite of veil (cover) . . . no.
6. **B.** "Candid (direct) is the opposite of furtive (secretive)."
   - A. Vain (pointless) is the opposite of futile (pointless) . . . no, they are synonyms.
   - B. Colossal (huge) is the opposite of infinitesimal (tiny) . . . yes!
   - C. Ostentatious (showy) is the opposite of showy . . . no, they are synonyms.
   - D. Recoil (flinch back) is the opposite of repress (restrain) . . . no.
   - E. Rue (regret) is the opposite of atone (regret) . . . no, they are synonyms.
7. **A.** "Fog *covered* the runway, and the passengers anticipated an imminent announcement from the captain postponing takeoff."
   Shrouded means *covered.* Notice the word *imminent,* which is a great vocabulary word that means *about to happen.* If there is a word in the sentence that you don't know, often you can work around it. Usually, SAT sentence completion questions are designed not to hinge on one word. So, if you see a word in the question that you don't know, rather than skip the question, ignore the word and see if you can still get the question right.
8. **B.** "Plans to move the *large* statue of Nero proved *impossible;* it was simply too large to transport."
   Colossal means *huge,* and *futile* means *pointless.* Use the process of elimination, one blank at a time.

His Topaz Eyes

Find each of the following words on the *Twilight* page number provided. Based on the way each word is used in the book, guess at its definition.

1. **Hyperactively** (p. 201) might mean _____

   _____

2. **Resigned** (p. 201) might mean _____

   _____

3. **Oblivious** (p. 207) might mean _____

   _____

4. **Faux** (p. 209) might mean _____

   _____

5. **Topaz** (p. 209) might mean _____

   _____

6. **Futilely** (p. 209) might mean _____

   _____

7. **Token** (p. 219) might mean _____

   _____

8. **Furtively** (p. 220) might mean _____

   _____

Let's see how you did. Check your answers, write the exact definitions, and reread the sentence in *Twilight* where each word appears. Then complete the drills.

1. **Hyperactively** (p. 201) means *overly actively*—remember from Group 3 that *hyper-* means *over* or *very*.

2. **Resigned** (p. 201) means *accepting defeat or some other undesirable result*. Mike wanted to date Bella, but has accepted that it's not a possibility—he is resigned. It's almost like **resigning** from a job that's too difficult.

3. **Oblivious** (p. 207) means *totally unaware*. This word is the opposite of *vigilant,* which means *watchful and attentive*.

4. **Faux** (p. 209) means *fake*. *Faux* is French for *false*. Let's look at this word in context. Bella is staring down at the " . . . faux wood grains printed on the laminate." Any wood grain that is printed is fake. That's enough to tell you that *faux* means *fake*. You can almost always figure out a tough word from its context!

5. **Topaz** (p. 209) in this case means *dark golden*. Topaz is a gemstone and can be colorless, yellow, or pale blue. You know, however, from the context that *topaz* refers to *dark golden* for two reasons. First, Edward's eyes are described on the previous page as "dark golden," and second, you know that Edward hunted only a few days earlier!

6. **Futilely** (p. 209) means *pointlessly*. You learned this word as a synonym for *vain* in Group 31.

7. **Token** (p. 219) in this case means *small*. It can also, of course, refer to a symbol, such as a rabbit's foot as a token of good luck.

8. **Furtively** (p. 220) means *secretively and nervously*. This is a great review of *surreptitiously* from way back in Group 5. The other synonyms were *clandestinely* and *covertly*.

Synonyms: Select the word or phrase whose meaning is closest to the word in capital letters.

Drills 🔑

1. RESIGNED
   A. hyperactive
   B. topaz
   C. surreptitious
   D. defeated
   E. candid

2. FAUX
   A. indulgent
   B. imminent
   C. fake
   D. fishtail
   E. furrowed

3. FUTILE
   A. vain
   B. shrouded
   C. belated
   D. ostentatious
   E. conspicuous

4. FURTIVE
   A. hyperactive
   B. fertile
   C. arable
   D. arboreal
   E. clandestine

Analogies: Select the answer choice that best completes the meaning of the sentence.

5. Industrious is to resigned as
   A. token is to colossal
   B. topaz is to russet
   C. faux is to oblivious
   D. pacify is to mollify
   E. assuage is to placate

6. Oblivious is to vigilant as
   A. unaware is to candid
   B. unconscious is to transparent
   C. unmindful is to circumspect
   D. pretentious is to blatant
   E. vampire is to werewolf

Sentence Completions: Choose the word that, when inserted in the sentence, best fits the meaning of the sentence as a whole.

7. Though he appeared resigned, Mike secretly held a(n) _____ amount of hope that one day he would date Bella.
   A. faux
   B. token
   C. hyperactive
   D. conspicuous
   E. unconditional

8. Many _____ children outgrow the symptoms of excessive energy and difficulty sitting still.
   A. resigned
   B. rueful
   C. complacent
   D. modulated
   E. hyperactive

1. **D.** *Resigned* means *accepting defeat,* so choice D is best. *Hyperactive* means *overly active, topaz* is *a gemstone that is often yellow, surreptitious* means *secretive,* and *candid* means *honest.*
2. **C.** *Faux* means *fake. Indulgent* means *decadent, imminent* means *coming soon,* and *furrowed* means *wrinkled.*
3. **A.** *Futile* and *vain* mean *pointless. Shrouded* means *covered, belated* means *late, ostentatious* means *showy,* and *conspicuous* means *obvious.*
4. **E.** *Furtive* and *clandestine* mean *secretive.* Use the process of elimination—cross off answers that you are sure don't work and choose the best of what's left. *Fertile* means *productive.* Did you remember *arable* (good for farming) and *arboreal* (pertaining to trees) from Group 10?
5. **A.** "Industrious (hard-working) is the opposite of resigned (accepting defeat)."
   - Ⓐ Token (small) is the opposite of colossal (huge) . . . yes.
   - B . Topaz (yellow gemstone) is the opposite of russet (reddish-brown) . . . no.
   - C . Faux (fake) is the opposite of oblivious (unaware) . . . no, they are unrelated.
   - D . Pacify (soothe) is the opposite of mollify (soothe) . . . no, they are synonyms.
   - E . Assuage (soothe) is the opposite of placate (soothe) . . . no, they are synonyms.
6. **C.** "Oblivious (unaware) is the opposite of vigilant (watchful)."
   - A . Unaware is the opposite of candid (honest) . . . no, they are unrelated.
   - B . Unconscious is the opposite of transparent (see-through) . . . no, they are unrelated.
   - Ⓒ Unmindful is the opposite of circumspect (wary) . . . yes.
   - D . Pretentious (showy) is the opposite of blatant (obvious) . . . no.
   - E . Vampire is the opposite of werewolf . . . no. Okay that was a trick; they may be sworn enemies, but they are not necessarily opposites.
7. **B.** "Though he appeared resigned, Mike secretly held a(n) _small_ amount of hope that one day he would date Bella."
   Token can mean *small.* Choice D, *conspicuous* (obvious), does not work because the sentence tells you that he appeared *resigned* (defeated).
8. **E.** "Many _excess energy_ children outgrow the symptoms of excessive energy and difficulty sitting still."
   Hyperactive means *excessively active. Modulated* means *regulated.*

A Deluge of Questions

Find each of the following words on the *Twilight* page number provided. Based on the way each word is used in the book, guess at its definition.

1. **Mercifully** (p. 220) might mean _____

   _____

2. **Vestiges** (p. 220) might mean _____

   _____

3. **Repentant** (p. 222) might mean _____

   _____

4. **Solemn** (p. 224) might mean _____

   _____

5. **Morosely** (p. 225) might mean _____

   _____

6. **Ambivalent** (p. 231) might mean _____

   _____

7. **Deluge** (p. 232) might mean _____

   _____

8. **Sparse** (p. 232) might mean _____

   _____

Let's see how you did. Check your answers, write the exact definitions, and reread the sentence in *Twilight* where each word appears. Then complete the drills.

1. **Mercifully** (p. 220) means *with mercy, fortunately,* or *thankfully*. It comes from the word *mercy,* which means *relief, compassion, or pity*. And, of course, in French, *merci* means *thank you*.

2. **Vestiges** (p. 220) means *remaining bits of something disappearing*. Synonym: remnants. In Biology class, you may have heard the related word *vestigial* to describe something that an animal has evolved to no longer need, such as wings for flightless ostriches.

3. **Repentant** (p. 222) means *regretful*. You saw this word in Group 11 as a synonym for *remorseful*. The other synonyms were *contrite* and *penitent*. This reminds me of a classic scene in *Indiana Jones and the Last Crusade,* where Indiana must pass through several traps to reach the Holy Grail. Approaching the first trap, he repeats the clue, " . . . only the penitent man will pass . . . " over and over until he realizes that a **penitent** man is **regretful** and humble and kneels before God. Indiana drops to his knees just in time to avoid a razor-sharp pendulum that slices his hat! (Paramount Pictures, 1989)

4. **Solemn** (p. 224) means *serious*. *Solemn* was a synonym for *sober* in Group 11, and for *grave* in Group 29. The other great synonym for *sober* was *somber*.

5. **Morosely** (p. 225) means *gloomily*. Morose was a synonym for *glum* in Group 9, *sullen* in Group 12, and *morbid* in Group 23. Some of the other great synonyms were *doleful, dour, lugubrious,* and *melancholic*. This page is all about review!

6. **Ambivalent** (p. 231) means *unsure* or *having mixed feelings*. Remember from Group 29 that *ambi-* means *both ways*. *Ambivalent* is *feeling both ways—having mixed feelings*. This word has the same meaning as the great SAT and ACT word *vacillating,* from Group 16.

7. **Deluge** (p. 232) means *flood* or *heavy rainfall*. Considering we are in Forks, Washington, on the Olympic Peninsula, I'm surprised that this is the first time we're seeing this word.

8. **Sparse** (p. 232) means *scattered* or *small amount of*.

Synonyms: Select the word or phrase whose meaning is closest to the word in capital letters.

1. MERCIFULLY
   A. seriously
   B. thankfully
   C. morosely
   D. ambivalently
   E. sparsely

2. REPENTANT
   A. rueful
   B. hyperactive
   C. resigned
   D. oblivious
   E. furtive

3. SOLEMN
   A. somber
   B. flooded
   C. contrite
   D. penitent
   E. serious

4. DELUGE
   A. faux
   B. vain
   C. colossal
   D. patent
   E. flood

Analogies: Select the answer choice that best completes the meaning of the sentence.

5. Vacillates is to ambivalent as
   A. encroaches is to humorous
   B. indulges is to nefarious
   C. abides is to disputing
   D. repents is to regretful
   E. circumvents is to scrutinizing

6. Morbid is to morose as
   A. glum is to jubilant
   B. sullen is to lugubrious
   C. dour is to elated
   D. doleful is to euphoric
   E. melancholic is to ecstatic

Sentence Completions: Choose the word that, when inserted in the sentence, <u>best</u> fits the meaning of the sentence as a whole.

7. After Nurmi dominated him in table tennis, Diego left the recreation center with few _____ of his former pride.
   A. mercies
   B. cadences
   C. vestiges
   D. taints
   E. tendrils

8. After the deluge, the pine grove grew from a(n) _____ populated stand of trees to a verdant forest.
   A. colossally
   B. mercifully
   C. solemnly
   D. ambivalently
   E. sparsely

1. **B.** *Mercifully* means *thankfully* or *fortunately*. *Morosely* means *gloomily*, *ambivalently* means *unsurely*, and *sparsely* means *thinly*.
2. **A.** *Repentant* and *rueful* mean *regretful*. *Hyperactive* means *very active*, *resigned* means *accepting defeat*, *oblivious* means *unaware*, and *furtive* means *secretive*.
3. **A.** *Solemn* and *somber* mean *serious*. *Contrite* and *penitent* mean *regretful*.
4. **E.** *Deluge* means *flood*. *Faux* means *false*, *vain* means *pointless*, *colossal* means *huge*, and *patent* means *obvious*.
5. **D.** "A person who vacillates is ambivalent."
   A. A person who encroaches (gradually advances) is humorous (funny) . . . no.
   B. A person who indulges is nefarious (wicked) . . . no, not necessarily.
   C. A person who abides (obeys) is disputing . . . no.
   D. A person who repents (regrets) is regretful . . . yes.
   E. A person who circumvents (avoids) is scrutinizing (carefully examining) . . . no.
6. **B.** "Morbid (gloomy) is very similar to morose (gloomy)."
   A. Glum (gloomy) is very similar to jubilant (psyched) . . . no, they are opposites.
   B. Sullen (gloomy) is very similar to lugubrious (gloomy) . . . yes.
   C. Dour (gloomy) is very similar to elated (psyched) . . . no, they are opposites.
   D. Doleful (gloomy) is very similar to euphoric (psyched) . . . no, they are opposites.
   E. Melancholic (gloomy) is very similar to ecstatic (psyched) . . . no, they are opposites.
7. **C.** "After Nurmi dominated him in table tennis, Diego left the recreation center with few <u>remnants</u> of his former pride."
   Vestiges means *leftovers* or *remnants*. *Cadences* means *rhythms*, *taints* means *contaminates*, and *tendrils* are *strands*.
8. **E.** "After the deluge, the pine grove grew from a(n) <u>thinly</u> populated stand of trees to a verdant forest."
   Sparsely means *thinly*. Remember that *verdant* from Group 10 means *lush and green*—like Forks, Washington, and not so much like Phoenix, Arizona.

A Growing Proximity

Find each of the following words on the *Twilight* page number provided. Based on the way each word is used in the book, guess at its definition.

1. **Monopolizing** (p. 232) might mean _____

_____

2. **Proximity** (p. 233) might mean _____

_____

3. **Hedged** (p. 239) might mean _____

_____

4. **Glowering** (p. 244) might mean _____

_____

5. **Willowy** (p. 246) might mean _____

_____

6. **Sinuous** (p. 247) might mean _____

_____

7. **Pretense** (p. 250) might mean _____

_____

8. **Insidious** (p. 251) might mean _____

_____

Let's see how you did. Check your answers, write the exact definitions, and reread the sentence in *Twilight* where each word appears. Then complete the drills.

1. **Monopolizing** (p. 232) means *having the largest portion of.* This word comes from the word *monopoly,* which means *control* or *sole ownership.* That's easy to remember since the goal in the game Monopoly is to gain control of all the properties on the board, from Baltic Avenue to Park Place. Remember from Group 4 that *mono-* means *one.* That's why *monopoly* means **one** *person controlling.*

2. **Proximity** (p. 233) means *nearness.* In Spanish, *proximo* means *next.* Synonym: propinquity.

3. **Hedged** (p. 239) in this case means *avoided making a definite statement.* It can also mean *qualified* (meaning *limited* or *made exceptions*). Helping you learn this word is one of my primary missions in this book—it appears very often on the SAT, ACT, and SSAT.

4. **Glowering** (p. 244) means *looking angry.* Saying the word *glowering* makes my face tense up—it even sounds angry and tense. Synonym: scowling.

5. **Willowy** (p. 246) means *slim and lithe.* Remember from Group 4 that *lithe* means *flexible and graceful?* The word *willowy* is easy to remember—it refers to the **thin, flexible** branches of a willow tree.

6. **Sinuous** (p. 247) means *lithe.* Let's review the great synonyms for Alice, I mean for *lithe:* agile, flexible, graceful, lissome, nimble, sinuous, supple, willowy.

7. **Pretense** (p. 250) means *false display.* Synonyms: facade, guise (like a superhero's disguise), pretext.

8. **Insidious** (p. 251) means *gradually progressing to harmful consequences.*

Synonyms: Select the word or phrase whose meaning is closest to the word in capital letters.

1. MONOPOLY
   A. proximity
   B. control
   C. hedge
   D. facade
   E. guise

2. PROPINQUITY
   A. proximity
   B. vestige
   C. ambivalence
   D. deluge
   E. futility

3. SINUOUS
   A. offhand
   B. cavalier
   C. flippant
   D. brusque
   E. lithe

4. INSIDIOUS
   A. cryptic
   B. enigmatic
   C. gradually harmful
   D. arcane
   E. recondite

Analogies: Select the answer choice that best completes the meaning of the sentence.

5. Faux is to facade as
   A. sinuous is to supple
   B. guise is to agile
   C. facade is to nimble
   D. pallid is to lissome
   E. glower is to gawk

6. Willowy is to burly as
   A. pariah is to outcast
   B. miffed is to irked
   C. inaudible is to muted
   D. finite is to eternal
   E. ominous is to menacing

Sentence Completions: Choose the word or words that, when inserted in the sentence, <u>best</u> fits the meaning of the sentence as a whole.

7. Jessica _____ the conversation, prattling nonstop in her usual _____ fashion.
   A. hedged . . laconic
   B. loathed . . sagacious
   C. circumvented . . sterile
   D. monopolized . . verbose
   E. evaded . . austere

8. Lithe and _____, Aurora looks like a gazelle when she races in cross-country meets.
   A. willowy
   B. insolent
   C. impudent
   D. impertinent
   E. audacious

1. **B.** *Monopoly* means *control. Proximity* means *nearness, hedge* means
   avoid making a definite statement, and *facade* and *guise* mean *a false*
   display.
2. **A.** *Propinquity* and *proximity* mean *nearness. Vestige* means *remainder,*
   ambivalence means *having mixed feelings, deluge* means *flood,* and
   futility means *pointlessness.*
3. **E.** *Sinuous* and *lithe* mean *graceful. Offhand, cavalier, flippant,* and
   brusque mean *offensively casual.*
4. **C.** *Insidious* means *gradually harmful. Cryptic, enigmatic, arcane,* and
   recondite mean *mysterious* or *difficult to understand.*
5. **A.** "Faux (fake) is similar to facade (false display)."
   - (**A.**) Sinuous is similar to supple . . . yes, they both mean *flexible.*
   - B. Guise (false display) is similar to agile (nimble) . . . no, they
     are unrelated.
   - C. Facade (false display) is similar to nimble . . . no, they are
     unrelated.
   - D. Pallid (pale) is similar to lissome (nimble) . . . no, they are
     unrelated.
   - E. Glower (stare at angrily) is similar to gawk (stare at blankly)
     . . . no, they are both looks, but very different looks.
6. **D.** "Willowy (thin and flexible) is the opposite of burly (bulky
   and muscular)."
   - A. Pariah is the opposite of outcast . . . no, they are synonyms.
   - B. Miffed is the opposite of irked . . . no, they both mean *mad.*
   - C. Inaudible is the opposite of muted . . . no, they both mean
     quiet.
   - (**D.**) Finite (limited) is the opposite of eternal (unlimited) . . . yes!
   - E. Ominous is the opposite of menacing . . . no, they both
     mean *threatening.*
7. **D.** "Jessica *dominated* the conversation, prattling nonstop in her
   usual *prattling* fashion."
   Great review. Let's look at the choices:
   - A. Hedged (avoided) . . laconic (brief)
   - B. Loathed (hated) . . sagacious (wise)
   - C. Circumvented (avoided) . . sterile (clean or uninspiring)
   - (**D.**) Monopolized (dominated) . . verbose (wordy)
   - E. Evaded (avoided) . . austere (harsh)
8. **A.** "Lithe and *lithe/gazelle-like,* Aurora looks like a gazelle when
   she races in cross-country meets."
   Willowy means *thin and lithe. Insolent, impudent,* and *impertinent*
   mean *rude. Audacious* means *bold* or *rude.*

Group 35
Incandescence

Find each of the following words on the *Twilight* page number provided. Based on the way each word is used in the book, guess at its definition.

1. **Condone** (p. 252) might mean _____

_____

2. **Impeccably** (p. 252) might mean _____

_____

3. **Nocturnes** (p. 252) might mean _____

_____

4. **Gratuitous** (p. 252) might mean _____

_____

5. **Martyred** (p. 253) might mean _____

_____

6. **Incandescent** (p. 260) might mean _____

_____

7. **Facets** (p. 262) might mean _____

_____

8. **Facade** (p. 264) might mean _____

_____

Let's see how you did. Check your answers, write the exact definitions, and reread the sentence in *Twilight* where each word appears. Then complete the drills.

1. **Condone** (p. 252) means *reluctantly approve or allow.* Synonym: sanction. *Condone* is the opposite of *condemn.*

2. **Impeccably** (p. 252) means *perfectly.*

3. **Nocturnes** (p. 252) means *musical compositions about the night.* That word will probably not be on your test, but the prefix *noct-,* which means *night,* might be. It helps you to understand great words such as *nocturnal* (at night) and *noctambulist* (a sleepwalker). *Ambul-* refers to *walk,* like in the word *amble* (stroll).

4. **Gratuitous** (p. 252) means *unwarranted.* I appreciate Stephenie Meyer's ability to capture our attention without resorting to **gratuitous** violence.

5. **Martyred** (p. 253) in this case means *a look of exaggerated discomfort to evoke sympathy.* It comes from the word *martyr,* which means *a person killed for his or her views.*

6. **Incandescent** (p. 260) in this case means *shining brightly.* It can also mean *giving off light when heated,* like a light bulb. These definitions are easy to remember since the word *incandescent* nearly has the word *candle* in it.

7. **Facets** (p. 262) means *sides,* like the faces of a cube. It can refer to the many facets of a diamond or to the several facets of a problem.

8. **Facade** (p. 264) means *false exterior.* It can also refer to *the exterior of a building.* This word comes from the French word for *face,* like the face of a building. You saw *facade* as a synonym for *pretense* in Group 34. The other synonyms were *guise* and *pretext.*

Synonyms: Select the word or phrase whose meaning is closest to the word in capital letters.

Drills

1. CONDONE
   A. converge
   B. allow
   C. chagrin
   D. mortify
   E. enunciate

2. NOCTURNAL
   A. petulant
   B. peevish
   C. wary
   D. nighttime
   E. chary

3. AMBLE
   A. err
   B. verify
   C. reproach
   D. veer
   E. saunter

4. FACETS
   A. threshold
   B. anemones
   C. affidavits
   D. sides
   E. eaves

Analogies: Select the answer choice that best completes the meaning of the sentence.

5. Impeccably is to unerringly as
   A. condone is to condemn
   B. sinuous is to burly
   C. insidious is to tainting
   D. facade is to pretense
   E. sparse is to myriad

6. Sanction is to forbid as
   A. literal is to verbatim
   B. hasty is to rushed
   C. tousled is to neat
   D. opaque is to solid
   E. terminate is to end

Sentence Completions: Choose the word that, when inserted in the sentence, best fits the meaning of the sentence as a whole.

7. Freda could not _____ the gratuitous drug use and violence in the film, so she rated it only one star.
   A. condone
   B. condemn
   C. monopolize
   D. hedge
   E. repent

8. Most bats and owls are _____, hunting primarily at night.
   A. arboreal
   B. incandescent
   C. martyrs
   D. nocturnal
   E. impeccable

1. **B.** *Condone* means *reluctantly accept or allow. Converge* means *meet up, chagrin* and *mortify* both mean *embarrass,* and *enunciate* means *speak clearly.*
2. **D.** *Nocturnal* means *nighttime. Petulant* and *peevish* mean *irritable. Wary* and *chary* mean *cautious.*
3. **E.** *Amble* and *saunter* both mean *walk casually. Err* means *be mistaken, verify* means *confirm, reproach* means *scold,* and *veer* means *change direction.*
4. **D.** *Facets* means *sides. Threshold* is *the floor under an entryway, anemones* are *sea creatures, affidavits* are *legal documents,* and *eaves* is *the overhang of a roof past a wall.*
5. **D.** "Impeccably (perfectly) is a synonym of unerringly (perfectly)."
   A . Condone (allow) is a synonym of condemn (criticize) . . . no, they are opposites.
   B . Sinuous (lithe) is a synonym of burly (muscular) . . . no, Alice is not a synonym of Emmett!
   C . Insidious (slowly harming) is a synonym of tainting (contaminating) . . . maybe, pretty close, but then the words in choice D turn out to be much more clearly synonymous.
   (D.) Facade (false display) is a synonym of pretense (false display) . . . definitely!
   E . Sparse (few) is a synonym of myriad (lots) . . . no, they are opposites.
6. **C.** "Sanction (allow) is the opposite of forbid."
   A . Literal (exact) is the opposite of verbatim (word for word) . . . no, they are synonyms.
   B . Hasty (rushed) is the opposite of rushed . . . no, they are synonyms.
   (C.) Tousled (messy) is the opposite of neat . . . yes.
   D . Opaque (solid) is the opposite of solid . . . no.
   E . Terminate (end) is the opposite of end . . . no.
7. **A.** "Freda could not <u>approve of</u> the gratuitous drug use and violence in the film, so she rated it only one star."
   Condone means *reluctantly approve or allow. Gratuitous* means *uncalled for.*
8. **D.** "Most bats and owls are <u>night creatures,</u> hunting primarily at night."
   Nocturnal means *nighttime. Arboreal* means *pertaining to trees.* Many bats and owls do like trees, but the phrase in the sentence after the blank describes the night, making choice D the best answer. Always choose an answer based on evidence in the question.

Quiz 7

I. Let's review some of the words that you've seen in Groups 31–35. Match each of the following words to the correct definition or synonym on the right. Then check the solutions on page 172.

1. Colossal	A.	Truthful
2. Candid	B.	Accepting defeat
3. Conspicuous	C.	Huge
4. Resigned	D.	Compassion
5. Oblivious	E.	Standing out
6. Furtive	F.	Serious
7. Mercy	G.	Total control
8. Solemn	H.	Unaware
9. Ambivalent	I.	Unsure
10. Monopoly	J.	Secretive
11. Sinuous	K.	Dangerous
12. Insidious	L.	Unwarranted
13. Condone	M.	Pretense
14. Gratuitous	N.	Reluctantly allow
15. Facade	O.	Lithe

II. Let's review several of the word parts that you've seen in Groups 31–35. Match each of the following word parts to the correct definition or synonym on the right. Then check the solutions on page 172.

16. Ambi-	A.	One
17. In-, Im-	B.	With
18. Con-	C.	Both ways
19. Noct-	D.	Over or very
20. Mono-	E.	Not
21. Hyper-	F.	Night

Group 36
Abstinence?

Find each of the following words on the *Twilight* page number provided. Based on the way each word is used in the book, guess at its definition.

1. **Ashen** (p. 264) might mean _____

_____

2. **Abstain** (p. 268) might mean _____

_____

3. **Contrite** (p. 269) might mean _____

_____

4. **Circuitous** (p. 271) might mean _____

_____

5. **Flippantly** (p. 275) might mean _____

_____

6. **Alleviate** (p. 275) might mean _____

_____

7. **Deplorable** (p. 277) might mean _____

_____

8. **Acerbic** (p. 283) might mean _____

_____

Let's see how you did. Check your answers, write the exact definitions, and reread the sentence in *Twilight* where each word appears. Then complete the drills.

Definitions

1. **Ashen** (p. 264) means *pale,* like the pale grayish color of ashes. This is a synonym for *pallid,* which you learned in Group 2. Another great synonym is *wan.*

2. **Abstain** (p. 268) means *refrain from doing,* something that Edward and Bella do . . . in so many ways.

3. **Contrite** (p. 269) means *regretful.* This was a synonym for *remorseful* in Group 11 and *repentant* in Group 33. The other synonym was *penitent*—think Indiana Jones!

4. **Circuitous** (p. 271) means *round about.* That's easy to remember, since *circuitous* sounds like *circle.*

5. **Flippantly** (p. 275) means *lacking seriousness. Flippant* was a synonym for *offhand* in Group 16. The other synonyms were *brusque, cavalier,* and *tactless.* Another great synonym is *facetious.*

6. **Alleviate** (p. 275) means *soothe* or *make less severe.* This word was a synonym for *appease* in Group 18 and *attenuated* in Group 20. Remember that the SAT absolutely **loves** using synonyms for *appeased.* The other synonyms for *appease* were *ameliorate, assuage, conciliate, mollify, pacify, palliate* (relieve but not cure), and *placate.* Another good one is *mitigate.*

7. **Deplorable** (p. 277) means *terrible. Deplore* means *disapprove of,* so *deplorable* means *something disapproved of.*

8. **Acerbic** (p. 283) means *sharp* or *cutting.* That's easy to remember since *acerbic* looks so much like *acidic.*

Synonyms: Select the word or phrase whose meaning is closest to the word in capital letters.

151

Drills

1. ASHEN
   A. contrite
   B. incandescent
   C. pale
   D. willowy
   E. glowering

2. ABSTAIN
   A. refrain
   B. repent
   C. resign
   D. shroud
   E. indulge

3. CONTRITE
   A. penitent
   B. conspicuous
   C. blatant
   D. patent
   E. colossal

4. FLIPPANT
   A. complacent
   B. recoiled
   C. unscathed
   D. inconsequential
   E. cavalier

Analogies: Select the answer choice that best completes the meaning of the sentence.

5. Acerbic is to tone as
   A. austere is to environment
   B. ashen is to color
   C. flippant is to attitude
   D. contrite is to facade
   E. gratuitous is to facet

6. Mitigate is to alleviate as
   A. palliate is to abstain
   B. assuage is to ameliorate
   C. mollify is to deplore
   D. placate is to condone
   E. pacify is to hedge

Sentence Completions: Choose the word that, when inserted in the sentence, best fits the meaning of the sentence as a whole.

7. More gray than white today, his ordinarily alabaster skin had a(n) _____ tone.
   A. ocher
   B. russet
   C. ashen
   D. auburn
   E. topaz

8. The route that they drove was so convoluted and _____ that no one could have followed them.
   A. circuitous
   B. ostentatious
   C. ambivalent
   D. dubious
   E. ubiquitous

1. **C.** *Ashen* means *pale. Contrite* means *regretful, incandescent* means *bright, willowy* means *lithe,* and *glowering* means *looking angrily.*

2. **A.** *Abstain* means *refrain. Abstain* is the opposite of *indulge.*

3. **A.** *Contrite* and *penitent* mean *regretful. Conspicuous, blatant,* and *patent* mean *obvious. Colossal* means *huge.*

4. **E.** *Flippant* and *cavalier* mean *lacking seriousness. Complacent* means *smug, recoiled* means *flinched back, unscathed* means *unharmed,* and *inconsequential* means *unimportant.*

5. **A.** "Acerbic is a harsh tone."
   - (**A.**) Austere is a harsh environment . . . yes.
   - B. Ashen is a harsh color . . . no, *ashen* is *a pale color.*
   - C. Flippant is a harsh attitude . . . no, *flippant* is *a non-serious attitude.*
   - D. Contrite (regretful) is a harsh facade (false display) . . . no, they are unrelated.
   - E. Gratuitous (unwarranted) is a harsh facet (side) . . . no, they are unrelated.

   Notice that the sentence "acerbic is a type of tone" is not specific enough to get the correct answer (since "ashen is a type of color" and "flippant is a type of attitude"). Be as specific as possible when creating your sentence.

6. **B.** "Mitigate (make less severe) means alleviate (make less severe)."
   - A. Palliate (make less severe) means abstain (refrain) . . . no.
   - (**B.**) Assuage (make less severe) means ameliorate (make less severe) . . . yes.
   - C. Mollify (make less severe) means deplore (disapprove of) . . . no.
   - D. Placate (make less severe) means condone (allow) . . . no.
   - E. Pacify (make less severe) means hedge (avoid) . . . no.

7. **C.** "More gray than white today, his ordinarily alabaster skin had a(n) *grayish* tone."

   Ashen means *pale gray.* Let's review the other colors. *Ocher* means *brownish-yellow. Auburn* and *russet* mean *reddish-brown,* and *topaz* can mean *golden.*

8. **A.** "The route that they drove was so convoluted and *convoluted* that no one could have followed them."

   Circuitous means *round about.* Let's review the other choices. *Ostentatious* means *showy, ambivalent* means *unsure, dubious* means *doubtful,* and *ubiquitous* means *all-present.*

Vampire Etiquette

Find each of the following words on the *Twilight* page number provided.
Based on the way each word is used in the book, guess at its definition.

1. **Seraphic** (p. 283) might mean _____

_____

2. **Buoyant** (p. 287) might mean _____

_____

3. **Chasm** (p. 303) might mean _____

_____

4. **Tenacity** (p. 307) might mean _____

_____

5. **Etiquette** (p. 318) might mean _____

_____

6. **Rhetorical** (p. 319) might mean _____

_____

7. **Relent** (p. 321) might mean _____

_____

8. **Reproving** (p. 325) might mean _____

_____

154 Let's see how you did. Check your answers, write the exact definitions, and reread the sentence in *Twilight* where each word appears. Then complete the drills.

1. **Seraphic** (p. 283) means *angelic*. Synonym: cherubic.

2. **Buoyant** (p. 287) in this case means *cheerful*. It can also mean *able to float*, like a buoy. You can see the connection—when someone is very cheerful, you might say, "She's floating on air."

3. **Chasm** (p. 303) means *deep gap*. Synonyms: abyss, schism.

4. **Tenacity** (p. 307) means *persistence* or *stubbornness*, like holding on tight. That makes sense since *tenacious* comes from the root *tenec-*, which means *to hold*. *Tenacious* was a synonym for *obstinate* in Group 27. The other synonyms were *intractable, obdurate, pertinacious* (stubborn and annoying), and *recalcitrant* (stubbornly uncooperative with authority).

5. **Etiquette** (p. 318) means *code of conduct*. There are codes for lots of venues. There's tennis court etiquette, Internet etiquette (netiquette), and even Facebook etiquette, like keeping pokes to a minimum.

6. **Rhetorical** (p. 319) in this case means *asked with no answer expected*. It can also refer to *the use of effective or convincing language*. The SAT and ACT like to use the word *rhetoric* to mean *style*, versus substance.

7. **Relent** (p. 321) means *stop* or *surrender*. Synonyms: abate, capitulate.

8. **Reproving** (p. 325) means *scolding*. It was a synonym for *condemn* in Group 5 and *reproach* in Group 18. The other synonyms were *censure, denounce,* and *rebuke*. Here's one more: *malicious* (mean) *condemnation* is called *vituperative*. The word *reproving* is easy to remember because when someone scolds, they often repeat themselves over and over again, **reproving** their point over and over (remember that *re-* means *again*, as in *resend*).

Synonyms: Select the word or phrase whose meaning is closest to the word in capital letters.

1. CHASM
   A. seraph
   B. buoy
   C. abyss
   D. martyr
   E. deluge

2. TENACIOUS
   A. intractable
   B. compendious
   C. byzantine
   D. palliative
   E. petulant

3. RHETORIC
   A. etiquette
   B. haste
   C. aerophobia
   D. abstraction
   E. style

4. REPROVE
   A. err
   B. vacillate
   C. waver
   D. scold
   E. loathe

Analogies: Select the answer choice that best completes the meaning of the sentence.

5. Tenacious is to relent as
   A. buoyant is to chortle
   B. contrite is to atone
   C. flippant is to joke
   D. glowering is to smile
   E. ambivalent is to waver

6. Rhetoric is to substance as
   A. chasm is to schism
   B. seraphic is to cherubic
   C. euphoric is to glum
   D. desolate is to anguished
   E. muddled is to befuddled

Sentence Completions: Choose the word that, when inserted in the sentence, <u>best</u> fits the meaning of the sentence as a whole.

7. His buoyant and affable manner caused many at the formal party to overlook his continual slips of _____.
   A. tenacity
   B. etiquette
   C. incandescence
   D. proximity
   E. mercy

8. Akshaya's _____ disposition was evident in her constant joy and her ability to see the best in all people.
   A. seraphic
   B. opaque
   C. compendious
   D. transcending
   E. vigorous

1. **C.** *Chasm* and *abyss* mean *deep gap*. *Seraph* means *angel, buoy* is a *float, martyr* is *one who dies for a belief,* and *deluge* means *flood.*

2. **A.** *Tenacious* and *intractable* mean *stubborn*. *Compendious* means *concise but complete, byzantine* means *complex, palliative* means *something that soothes,* and *petulant* means *irritable.*

3. **E.** *Rhetoric* means *style*. *Etiquette* means *code of conduct, haste* means *rushing, aerophobia* means *fear of flying,* and *abstraction* means *thoughts.*

4. **D.** *Reprove* means *scold*. *Err* means *make an error, vacillate* means *waver,* and *loathe* means *hate.*

5. **D.** "Tenacious (stubborn) people do not relent (give in)."
   A. Buoyant (cheerful) people do not chortle (chuckle) . . . no, they probably do.
   B. Contrite (repentant) people do not atone (repent) . . . no, they do.
   C. Flippant (not serious) people do not joke . . . no, they probably do.
   (D.) Glowering (angry looking) people do not smile . . . true.
   E. Ambivalent (unsure) people do not waver . . . no, they probably do.

6. **C.** "Rhetoric can be the opposite of substance."
   A. Chasm (deep gap) can be the opposite of schism (a split) . . . no.
   B. Seraphic (angelic) can be the opposite of cherubic (angelic) . . . no.
   (C.) Euphoric (elated) can be the opposite of glum (sad) . . . yes.
   D. Desolate (miserable) can be the opposite of anguished (pained) . . . no.
   E. Muddled (confused) can be the opposite of befuddled (confused) . . . no.

7. **B.** "His buoyant and affable manner caused many at the formal party to overlook his continual slips of *formality*."
   Etiquette means *code of conduct. Buoyant* means *cheery,* and *affable* means *friendly.* If you can't think of a word to fill the blank before you look at the choices, then try the choices and use the process of elimination. "**Formal** party" tells you that *etiquette* is the best answer. *Incandescence* means *brightness, proximity* means *nearness,* and *mercy* means *compassion.*

8. **A.** "Akshaya's *joyful/generous* disposition was evident in her constant joy and her ability to see the best in all people."
   Seraphic means *angelic. Opaque* means *solid, compendious* means *concise but complete, transcending* means *going beyond,* and *vigorous* means *energetic.*

A Poignant Past

Find each of the following words on the *Twilight* page number provided. Based on the way each word is used in the book, guess at its definition.

1. **Profusion** (p. 326) might mean _____

2. **Tyrant** (p. 328) might mean _____

3. **Melancholy** (p. 329) might mean _____

4. **Poignantly** (p. 329) might mean _____

5. **Monochromes** (p. 335) might mean _____

6. **Seventeenth-century** (p. 336) might mean _____

7. **Impassive** (p. 337) might mean _____

8. **Vile** (p. 337) might mean _____

Let's see how you did. Check your answers, write the exact definitions, and reread the sentence in *Twilight* where each word appears. Then complete the drills.

Definitions

1. **Profusion** (p. 326) means *large amount*. *Profusion* comes from the word *profuse*, which also means *a large amount*. Synonyms: abundance, cornucopia (large amount of good things).

2. **Tyrant** (p. 328) means *cruel and harsh leader*. Stalin, Napoleon, Mussolini, Big Brother (George Orwell's *1984*), and Lord Voldemort (J. K. Rowling's *Harry Potter* series) are a few famous tyrants of history.

3. **Melancholy** (p. 329) means *sad*. It was a synonym for *glum, morose,* and *sullen* in earlier groups. The other synonyms were *doleful, dour,* and *lugubrious*. I remember this word because it sounds like *mellow,* which is how I feel when I'm sad.

4. **Poignantly** (p. 329) means *evoking bittersweet feelings*. *Poignantly* sounds like *pointedly,* which is not a coincidence because *poignantly* comes from the word *prick,* piercing one's heart.

5. **Monochromes** (p. 335) in this case means *pictures in shades of one color*. In Group 4, you learned that *mono-* means *one*. And *-chrom* implies *color*.

6. **Seventeenth-century** (p. 336) means *the years 1600–1699*. I have seen this throw students in the reading passages on standardized tests. The years are always one number lower than the century number, for example *the twenty-first century* means *the years 2000–2099*. This is also a great time to mention that *cent-* means *one hundred*, as in *centipede* (a tiny invertebrate with one hundred legs).

7. **Impassive** (p. 337) means *expressionless*.

8. **Vile** (p. 337) means *terrible* or *wicked*. Synonyms: baleful, depraved, heinous, impious, iniquitous, malevolent, menacing, nefarious, pernicious, sinister.

Synonyms: Select the word or phrase whose meaning is closest to the word in capital letters.

1. PROFUSE
   A. tyrannical
   B. dour
   C. doleful
   D. abundant
   E. lugubrious

2. MELANCHOLY
   A. morose
   B. multihued
   C. seraphic
   D. buoyant
   E. tenacious

3. IMPASSIVE
   A. relenting
   B. inexpressive
   C. capitulating
   D. abating
   E. ashen

4. VILE
   A. poignant
   B. contrite
   C. terrible
   D. acerbic
   E. impeccable

Analogies: Select the answer choice that best completes the meaning of the sentence.

5. Tyrant is to mercy as
   A. chasm is to depth
   B. facade is to pretense
   C. martyr is to audacity
   D. seraph is to evil
   E. monopoly is to control

6. Monochrome is to multihued as
   A. poignant is to sterile
   B. vile is to pernicious
   C. wicked is to nefarious
   D. depraved is to heinous
   E. impious is to sinister

Sentence Completions: Choose the word that, when inserted in the sentence, <u>best</u> fits the meaning of the sentence as a whole.

7. In the seventeenth century, audacious individuals ventured to foreign lands seeking religious freedom and fleeing religious _____.
   A. profusion
   B. tyranny
   C. impassivity
   D. alleviation
   E. mitigation

8. Many photographers find the nostalgia and subtlety of _____ black-and-white photos more poignant than color photos.
   A. vile
   B. relenting
   C. reproving
   D. deplorable
   E. monochromatic

1. **D.** *Profuse* and *abundant* mean *plentiful*. *Tyrannical* means *cruel and harsh;* and *dour, doleful,* and *lugubrious* mean *sad*.

2. **A.** *Melancholy* and *morose* mean *sad*. *Multihued* means *many-colored, seraphic* means *angelic, buoyant* means *cheerful,* and *tenacious* means *stubborn*.

3. **B.** *Impassive* means *inexpressive*. *Relenting, capitulating,* and *abating* mean *surrendering*. *Ashen* means *pale gray,* like the color of ash.

4. **C.** *Vile* means *terrible or wicked*. *Poignant* means *touching, contrite* means *remorseful, acerbic* means *cutting,* and *impeccable* means *perfect*.

5. **D.** "A tyrant (cruel leader) lacks mercy (compassion)."
   - A. A chasm (deep gap) lacks depth . . . no.
   - B. A facade (false display) lacks pretense (false display) . . . no.
   - C. A martyr (person who dies for beliefs) lacks audacity (bravery) . . . no, probably not.
   - (D.) A seraph (angel) lacks evil . . . yes.
   - E. A monopoly (exclusive control) lacks control . . . no.

6. **A.** "Monochrome (one color) is the opposite of multihued (many-colored)."
   - (A.) Poignant (touching) is the opposite of sterile (uninspiring) . . . maybe.
   - B. Vile is the opposite of pernicious . . . no, they both mean *wicked*.
   - C. Wicked is the opposite of nefarious . . . no, they both mean *wicked*.
   - D. Depraved is the opposite of heinous . . . no, they both mean *wicked*.
   - E. Impious is the opposite of sinister . . . no, they both mean *wicked*.

   All of these words for *wicked* even sound evil. *Impious* is a cool word to break apart. *Im-* means *not,* and *pious* means *good, loyal,* or *religious,* so *impious* means *not good—wicked*. Choice A is not ideal, but by using the process of elimination, you can see that it's better than the others.

7. **B.** "In the seventeenth century, audacious individuals ventured to foreign lands seeking religious freedom and fleeing religious _non-freedom._"

   Tyranny means *cruel and harsh leadership*.

8. **E.** "Many photographers find the nostalgia and subtlety of _????_ black-and-white photos more poignant than color photos."

   On the rare occasion that you can't think of a word to fill the blank, try the choices. *Monochromatic,* meaning *one-colored,* is the best choice.

An Ominous Gait

Find each of the following words on the *Twilight* page number provided.
Based on the way each word is used in the book, guess at its definition.

1. **Reverent** (p. 339) might mean _____

   _____

2. **Blatant** (p. 345) might mean _____

   _____

3. **Vivid** (p. 347) might mean _____

   _____

4. **Bracken** (p. 364) might mean _____

   _____

5. **Tersely** (p. 372) might mean _____

   _____

6. **Apathy** (p. 374) might mean _____

   _____

7. **Gait** (p. 375) might mean _____

   _____

8. **Urbane** (p. 376) might mean _____

   _____

Let's see how you did. Check your answers, write the exact definitions, and reread the sentence in *Twilight* where each word appears. Then complete the drills.

1. **Reverent** (p. 339) means *deeply respectful.* Almost everyone treats Carlisle reverently. This word is easy to remember; it sounds like *Reverend*—a minister.

2. **Blatant** (p. 345) means *obvious. Blatant* was a synonym for *conspicuous* in Group 31. The other synonym was *patent.*

3. **Vivid** (p. 347) means *lively, bright,* or *clear.* That makes sense, since in Spanish the verb *vivir* means *to live.* "*Vive los vampiros!*"

4. **Bracken** (p. 364) means *ferns.* I lived near the Olympic Peninsula for one year, and there were a *plethora* (myriad, profusion) of ferns. They love the damp shade. Bella falls a lot, so she must get a lot of mud and bracken on the back of her jacket.

5. **Tersely** (p. 372) means *briefly. Terse* was a synonym for *curt* (brief and rude) in Group 27. The other synonyms (also more rude) were *brusque, laconic,* and *surly* (hostile).

6. **Apathy** (p. 374) means *lack of interest.* Remember from Group 27 that *a-* means *without* and *path* refers to *feeling.* This word was a synonym for *indifferent* in Group 28. The other synonym was *dispassionate.*

7. **Gait** (p. 375) means *style of walking,* like a horse's gait. This word was particularly clear in the context of the sentence, "Their walk was catlike . . . " Remember to look at the context when you see a word that you don't know; usually you can determine its meaning. You've seen a bunch of gaits in this workbook—sauntering, flitting, shambling, lumbering, and ambling.

8. **Urbane** (p. 376) means *courteous and refined.* This word comes from the word *urban,* meaning *city,* from the notion that city folk are polished and refined. James, Laurent, and Victoria stood like animals, while Carlisle stood like the refined gentleman that he is.

Synonyms: Select the word or phrase whose meaning is closest to the word in capital letters.

1. REVERENT
   A. offhand
   B. flippant
   C. cavalier
   D. brusque
   E. respectful

2. BLATANT
   A. subtle
   B. muted
   C. surreptitious
   D. obvious
   E. furtive

3. TERSE
   A. verbose
   B. brief
   C. apathetic
   D. vivid
   E. rhetorical

4. URBANE
   A. polished
   B. tyrannical
   C. impassive
   D. vile
   E. melancholy

Analogies: Select the answer choice that best completes the meaning of the sentence.

5. Amble is to gait as
   A. vivid is to color
   B. tyrant is to leader
   C. vile is to reverence
   D. etiquette is to chasm
   E. vampire is to seraph

6. Terse is to verbose as
   A. urbane is to impudent
   B. lancet is to surgeon
   C. alluring is to appealing
   D. menacing is to
      threatening
   E. inept is to incompetent

Sentence Completions: Choose the word that, when inserted in the sentence, <u>best</u> fits the meaning of the sentence as a whole.

7. Maria rarely seems
   _____; her vivid
   expression and eager gait
   blatantly demonstrate her
   excitement.
   A. reverent
   B. terse
   C. urbane
   D. apathetic
   E. solitary

8. Rui has a deep _____ for
   nature and steps carefully
   to avoid the bracken on the
   forest floor.
   A. reverence
   B. menace
   C. abhorrence
   D. scorn
   E. malice

1. **E.** *Reverent* means *deeply respectful. Offhand, flippant, cavalier,* and *brusque* mean *disrespectfully casual.*

2. **D.** *Blatant* means *obvious. Subtle, muted, surreptitious,* and *furtive* all mean *not obvious.*

3. **B.** *Terse* means *brief. Verbose* means *wordy, apathetic* means *not caring, vivid* means *bright,* and *rhetorical* means *stylistic.*

4. **A.** *Urbane* means *polished. Tyrannical* means *oppressively controlling, impassive* means *not divulging, vile* means *terrible,* and *melancholy* means *sad.*

5. **B.** "Amble is a type of gait."
   A . Vivid is a type of color . . . no, *vivid* means *bright.*
   (B.) Tyrant (oppressive leader) is a type of leader . . . yes.
   C . Vile (terrible) is a type of reverence (respect) . . . no.
   D . Etiquette (conduct) is a type of chasm (deep gap) . . . no, they are unrelated.
   E . Vampire is a type of seraph (angel) . . . depends which vampire.
   I told you to make your sentence as specific as possible. However, sometimes a sentence might not work for any of the choices. For example, "amble is a relaxed gait" is an excellent sentence, more specific than "amble is a type of gait," but no answer would seem to work. When that happens, reword your sentence or choose the closest answer choice.

6. **A.** "Terse (brief) is the opposite of verbose (wordy)."
   (A.) Urbane (polished) is the opposite of impudent (rude) . . . yes.
   B . Lancet (surgical knife) is the opposite of surgeon . . . no, a lancet is used by a surgeon.
   C . Alluring (appealing) is the opposite of appealing . . . no.
   D . Menacing (threatening) is the opposite of threatening . . . no.
   E . Inept (incompetent) is the opposite of incompetent . . . no.

7. **D.** "Maria rarely seems *not excited;* her vivid expression and eager gait blatantly demonstrate her excitement."
   Apathetic means *not interested.*

8. **A.** "Rui has a deep *care/respect* for nature and steps carefully to avoid the bracken on the forest floor."
   Reverence means *respect.*

Thwarted Enmity

Find each of the following words on the *Twilight* page number provided. Based on the way each word is used in the book, guess at its definition.

1. **Genial** (p. 378) might mean _____

   _____

2. **Ruse** (p. 387) might mean _____

   _____

3. **Thwarted** (p. 397) might mean _____

   _____

4. **Balefully** (p. 399) might mean _____

   _____

5. **Enmity** (p. 400) might mean _____

   _____

6. **Benign** (p. 407) might mean _____

   _____

7. **Glut** (p. 413) might mean _____

   _____

8. **Superfluous** (p. 413) might mean _____

   _____

Let's see how you did. Check your answers, write the exact definitions, and reread the sentence in *Twilight* where each word appears. Then complete the drills.

1. **Genial** (p. 378) means *friendly*. Synonyms: affable, amiable, amicable.

2. **Ruse** (p. 387) means *trick*.

3. **Thwarted** (p. 397) means *prevented*. Synonym: stymied. *Stymie* was originally a golfing term for when one ball blocked (prevented) the shot of another player.

4. **Balefully** (p. 399) means *threateningly*. Baleful was a synonym for *sinister* in Group 23 and *vile* in Group 38. The other synonyms were *depraved, heinous, impious, iniquitous, malevolent, menacing, nefarious,* and *pernicious*.

5. **Enmity** (p. 400) means *opposition* or *hostility*. That's easy to remember since the word *enmity* looks so similar to *enemy*. Synonyms: animosity, antipathy. *Antipathy* is a cool word to break apart. *Anti-* means *against,* and you know that *path-* refers to *feeling,* so *antipathy* means *feeling against*—opposing, disliking.

6. **Benign** (p. 407) means *kindly* or *harmless*. This word is used in medicine (a benign tumor is harmless, and a malignant tumor is cancerous), so you hear it regularly on *Scrubs, House,* and *Grey's Anatomy*.

7. **Glut** (p. 413) means *excessive supply*. Synonyms: plethora, surfeit. *Surfeit* sounds like *surplus,* which is exactly what it means.

8. **Superfluous** (p. 413) means *unnecessary* or *more than needed*. *Superfluous* is an interesting word to break apart. *Super-* means *over* or *beyond,* like Superman, and *flu* refers to *flow*. So *superfluous* means *over flow*—*more than needed*. I talked about this word in the drill solutions for Group 9—the scene in *Pirates of the Caribbean: The Curse of the Black Pearl* when Johnny Depp's character is about to steal a ship. Check it out!

Synonyms: Select the word or phrase whose meaning is closest to the word in capital letters.

1. GENIAL
   A. affable
   B. baleful
   C. menacing
   D. malevolent
   E. pernicious

2. THWART
   A. trick
   B. revere
   C. stymie
   D. relent
   E. abstain

3. ENMITY
   A. immersion
   B. apathy
   C. poignancy
   D. buoyancy
   E. animosity

4. SUPERFLUOUS
   A. industrious
   B. unnecessary
   C. conscientious
   D. sedulous
   E. assiduous

Analogies: Select the answer choice that best completes the meaning of the sentence.

5. Genial is to frigid as
   A. thwart is to prevent
   B. benign is to harmless
   C. superfluous is to necessary
   D. glut is to surfeit
   E. plethora is to myriad

6. Enemy is to enmity as
   A. adversary is to amicable
   B. magician is to ruse
   C. tyrant is to remorse
   D. friend is to amity
   E. opponent is to camaraderie

Sentence Completions: Choose the word or phase that, when inserted in the sentence, best fits the meaning of the sentence as a whole.

7. Considering a vampire's charm, speed, and strength, many consider its venom _____; an unnecessary extra weapon.
   A. stipulated
   B. superfluous
   C. benign
   D. a facade
   E. a guise

8. High winds and impending snow _____ the airline's attempts to stay on schedule, delaying all flights.
   A. thwarted
   B. alleviated
   C. condoned
   D. sanctioned
   E. monopolized

1. **A.** *Genial* and *affable* mean *friendly*. *Baleful, menacing, malevolent,* and *pernicious* mean *threatening* or *harmful*.

2. **C.** *Thwart* and *stymie* mean *prevent*. Choice A, the word *trick,* is a bit of a trick. A trick might prevent something from happening, but *thwart* does not directly mean *trick,* it means *prevent*. *Revere* means *respect, relent* means *surrender,* and *abstain* means *refrain from*.

3. **E.** *Enmity* means *opposition* or *hostility*. That's also what *animosity* means. *Immersion* means *submersion, apathy* means *lack of interest, poignancy* refers to *sentimentality,* and *buoyancy* means *cheerfulness*.

4. **B.** *Superfluous* means *unnecessary*. *Industrious, conscientious, sedulous,* and *assiduous* mean *diligent and hard-working*.

5. **C.** "Genial (friendly) is the opposite of frigid (unfriendly)."
   A. Thwart (prevent) is the opposite of prevent . . . no.
   B. Benign (harmless) is the opposite of harmless . . . no.
   C. Superfluous (unnecessary) is the opposite of necessary . . . yes.
   D. Glut (surplus) is the opposite of surfeit (surplus) . . . no, they are synonyms.
   E. Plethora (surplus) is the opposite of myriad (a lot) . . . no, they are very similar.

6. **D.** "An enemy feels enmity (opposition)."
   A. An adversary (opponent) feels amicable (friendly) . . . no, not necessarily.
   B. A magician feels ruse (trick) . . . no, a magician uses a ruse.
   C. A tyrant (oppressive ruler) feels remorse (regret) . . . no, not necessarily.
   D. A friend feels amity (friendship) . . . yes.
   E. An opponent feels camaraderie (deep friendship) . . . no, not necessarily.

7. **B.** "Considering a vampire's charm, speed, and strength, many consider its venom <u>unnecessary</u>; an unnecessary extra weapon."
   Superfluous means *unnecessary*. *Stipulated* means *required,* and *benign* means *harmless*. The sentence does not say that venom is harmless, just that it is extra. *Facade* and *guise* both mean *false display*.

8. **A.** "High winds and impending snow <u>delayed</u> the airline's attempts to stay on schedule, delaying all flights."
   Thwarted means *prevented*. *Alleviated* means *relieved, condoned* means *allowed, sanctioned* means *allowed,* and *monopolized* means *controlled*. *Controlled* almost works, but *prevented* is a more logically flowing choice.

Quiz 8

I. Let's review some of the words that you've seen in Groups 36–40. Match each of the following words to the correct definition or synonym on the right. Then check the solutions on page 172.

1. Contrite		A. Placate
2. Flippant		B. Persistence
3. Alleviate		C. Penitent
4. Tenacity		D. Reproach
5. Rhetoric		E. Offhand
6. Reprove		F. Abundant
7. Profuse		G. Respectful
8. Melancholy		H. Refined
9. Vile		I. Style
10. Reverent		J. Unnecessary
11. Terse		K. Stymie
12. Urbane		L. Morose
13. Genial		M. Affable
14. Thwart		N. Sinister
15. Superfluous		O. Laconic

II. Let's review several of the word parts that you've seen in Groups 36–40. Match each of the following word parts to the correct definition or synonym on the right. Then check the solutions on page 172.

16. Cent-		A. Against
17. Re-		B. One hundred
18. Mono-		C. Feeling
19. Path-		D. Over or beyond
20. Anti-		E. Again
21. Super-		F. One

Review

Match each group of synonyms to its general meaning. Then check the solutions on page 172.

1. Baleful
   Depraved
   Heinous
   Impious
   Iniquitous
   Malevolent
   Nefarious
   Pernicious
   Sinister

   A. Passionate

2. Assiduous
   Conscientious
   Diligent
   Industrious
   Sedulous

   B. Wicked

3. Intractable
   Obdurate
   Obstinate
   Pertinacious
   Recalcitrant
   Tenacious

   C. Hard-working

4. Ardent
   Avid
   Fervent
   Keen
   Zealous

   D. Friendly

5. Affable
   Amiable
   Amicable
   Genial

   E. Stubborn

Quiz and Review Solutions

Quiz 1	Quiz 2	Quiz 3	Quiz 4	Groups 1–20 Review
1. G	1. C	1. C	1. B	1. C
2. H	2. F	2. D	2. D	2. D
3. N	3. H	3. A	3. A	3. E
4. C	4. A	4. F	4. G	4. F
5. I	5. I	5. J	5. H	5. A
6. M	6. B	6. E	6. C	6. B
7. D	7. G	7. K	7. K	
8. O	8. K	8. B	8. L	
9. L	9. D	9. G	9. E	
10. E	10. L	10. H	10. F	
11. K	11. N	11. L	11. I	
12. F	12. O	12. I	12. N	
13. J	13. M	13. O	13. J	
14. A	14. E	14. M	14. M	
15. B	15. J	15. N	15. O	
16. D	16. D	16. C	16. E	
17. E	17. F	17. F	17. D	
18. B	18. B	18. B	18. F	
19. C	19. E	19. D	19. A	
20. A	20. A	20. A	20. C	
21. F	21. C	21. E	21. B	

Quiz 5	Quiz 6	Quiz 7	Quiz 8	Groups 21–40 Review
1. I	1. E	1. C	1. C	1. B
2. A	2. D	2. A	2. E	2. C
3. M	3. A	3. E	3. A	3. E
4. B	4. G	4. B	4. B	4. A
5. H	5. B	5. H	5. I	5. D
6. K	6. I	6. J	6. D	
7. C	7. C	7. D	7. F	
8. D	8. K	8. F	8. L	
9. L	9. F	9. I	9. N	
10. E	10. H	10. G	10. G	
11. J	11. O	11. O	11. O	
12. F	12. N	12. K	12. H	
13. G	13. J	13. N	13. M	
14. O	14. L	14. L	14. K	
15. N	15. M	15. M	15. J	
16. C	16. C	16. C	16. B	
17. E	17. A	17. E	17. E	
18. F	18. F	18. B	18. F	
19. B	19. B	19. F	19. C	
20. A	20. D	20. A	20. A	
21. D	21. E	21. D	21. D	

Glossary

Abhorred hated. Synonyms: *despised, loathed, scorned*

Abide by obey

Abstain refrain from doing

Abstraction thoughts, preoccupation. Synonym: *pensiveness*

Acerbic sharp, cutting

Adroit dexterous and skilled

Affidavits written statements sworn under oath

Alabaster a translucent, white mineral

Alleviate soothe, make less severe

Alluring appealing and charming

Ambivalent unsure, having mixed feelings

Amended added to correct or improve

Amorphous without clear shape, vague

Anemones sea animals that attach to rock or coral

Anguished pained

Animatedly energetically

Antagonistic hostile

Apathy lack of interest. Synonyms: *dispassionate, indifferent*

Appalled greatly distressed

Appeased satisfied, pleased. Synonyms for appease: *alleviate, ameliorate, assuage, conciliate, mollify, pacify, palliate, placate*

Apprehensively uneasily, anxiously

Arable good for farming, such as arable land

Arboreal relating to trees

Ashen pale. Synonyms: *pallid, wan*

Astute using wisdom for one's own benefit

Attenuated thinned or lessened, soothed

Auburn reddish-brown

Austere harsh, very strict, or very plain. Synonyms: *severe, stark*

Automatically happening by itself, without conscious intention

Averting turning away

Balefully threateningly

Bedlam noise and confusion. Synonyms: *anarchy, chaos, mayhem, pandemonium, turmoil*

Befuddled unable to think clearly. Synonyms: *addled, muddled*

Belatedly later than it should have

Benign kindly, harmless

Blaring loud and harsh

Blatant obvious. Synonym: *patent*

Bleak cold and forbidding

Bouquets beautiful groupings

Bracken ferns

Briny salty

Broach approach, raise for discussion

Bulbous rounded, bulging

Buoyant cheerful or able to float

Burly large and muscular

By dint of because of (usually used when an action requires force)

Cadences rhythms

Camaraderie warmth and friendship. Synonym: *amity*

Candid upfront and truthful. Synonyms: *blunt, frank, sincere*

Catastrophes disasters

Ceaselessly endlessly. Synonyms: *eternally, incessantly, interminably, relentlessly*

Chagrin embarrassment. Synonym: *mortification*

Chaotically with complete disorder and confusion

Chasm deep gap. Synonyms: *abyss, schism*

Chivalrously courteously and bravely. Synonym: *gallant*

Chortling a mixture of the words chuckling and snorting

Circuitous round about

Circumnavigate sail around

Circumspect cautious

Circumvent go around, avoid

Clamorous loudly protesting

Claustrophobia fear of confined spaces

Coherently in a clear, logical, and consistent way. Synonym for coherent: *lucid*

Colossal huge

Commercial industrial, business-related

Communal shared

Compendious comprehensive but concise

Compilation grouping

Complacent smug and self-satisfied

Complimentary giving compliments, free

Concealment hiding

Condemnation strong disapproval. Synonyms for condemn: *censure, denounce, rebuke, reproach, reprove*

Condescendingly with superiority. Synonym: *patronizingly*

Condone reluctantly approve or allow. Synonym: *sanction*

Conspicuous clearly visible, standing out. Synonyms: *blatant, patent*

Constructive useful

Constructs theories

Contrite regretful

Converge approach and join together

Convoluted complicated and difficult to follow. Synonyms: *byzantine, elaborate*

Convulsively with a sudden, involuntary movement

Coy intentionally or even manipulatively cute, warm, and attentive

Cryptic mysterious. Synonyms: *abstruse, ambiguous, arcane, enigmatic, oracular, recondite*

Curb restrain

Curtly in a brief and sharp way. Synonyms for curt: *abrupt, brusque, gruff, laconic, surly, terse*

Dazzle stun with charm, skills, or appeal

Dejected made sad

Deliberately on purpose, with care

Deluge flood, heavy rainfall

Deplorable terrible

Derision harsh mockery. Synonyms: *disparagement, ridicule, scorn*

Desolation total emptiness or misery

Despair misery, hopelessness. Synonyms: *anguish, desolation, despondency, wretchedness*

Despise hate. Synonyms: *abhor, detest, disdain, loathe, scorn*

Detested hated a lot

Diplomacy dealing with people in a sensitive way. Synonyms: *mediation, suave, tact*

Disheveled messy

Disparaging disapproving. Synonyms: *censorious, reproachful*

Donned put on (usually clothes)

Dredged up brought up

Droned spoke in a dull, monotonous tone

Dubious doubtful, hesitant

Eaves the part of a roof that hangs over the side of a house

Ebb reduce, recede. Synonym: *wane*

Egotistical self-centered. Synonyms: *narcissistic, solipsistic, vain*

Elated very psyched. Synonyms: *ecstatic, euphoric, jubilant, rapturous*

Emanating radiating

Encroaching intruding, advancing

Enigmatic mysterious

Enmity opposition, hostility. Synonyms: *animosity, antipathy*

Enunciated pronounced clearly

Erratic inconsistent, unpredictable. Synonyms: *arbitrary, capricious, fickle, impetuous, sporadic, whimsical*

Estrogen female hormones, female bonding

Etiquette code of conduct

Euphoric thrilled. Synonyms: *ecstatic, elated, jubilant, rapturous*

Evaded avoided. Synonyms for evade: *circumvent, elude, equivocate, prevaricate*

Exiled sent away, banished

Exponentially more and more rapidly

Facade false exterior, the exterior of a building. Synonyms: *guise, pretense, pretext*

Facets sides

Fathom understand, comprehend

Faux fake

Fervent passionate. Synonyms: *ardent, avid, fervid, keen, vehement, zealous*

Finite limited

Fishtailed moved sideways

Flippantly lacking seriousness. Synonym: *facetiousness*

Flitted moved quickly

Floundered struggled uncomfortably

Flourish an exaggerated gesture, a decorative curve in handwriting, to thrive

Frigidly coldly, not friendly. Synonyms: *callously, frostily, impersonally*

Furrowed wrinkled from frowning

Furtively secretively and nervously. Synonyms: *clandestinely, covertly, surreptitiously*

Futilely pointlessly

Gait style of walking

Gallant brave

Gawked stared stupidly. Synonym: *gaped*

Genial friendly. Synonyms: *affable, amiable, amicable*

Glowering looking angry. Synonym: *scowling*

Glum sad. Synonyms: *doleful, dour, lugubrious, melancholic, morose, sullen*

Glut excessive supply. Synonyms: *plethora, surfeit*

Gratuitous unwarranted

Grave serious, solemn

Gruff grouchy

Hastily hurriedly

Haven a place of safety or comfort

Hedged avoided making a definite statement or made exceptions

Histrionic theatrical, very dramatic

Hostile very unfriendly

Husbandry care of crops, animals, or the environment

Hyperactively overly actively

Hyperventilation breathing overly fast

Hypothetically in theory

Hysterics a very emotional reaction, uncontrollable laughter

Immersed engrossed, submerged

Impassive expressionless

Impeccably perfectly

Impenetrable impossible to enter or understand

Imperative very important

Inaudible not hearable

Incandescent shining brightly

Incapacitate paralyze. Synonym: *debilitate*

Inconsequential not important

Inconspicuously not conspicuously, discreetly

Incredulous unbelieving

Indecisive not decisive, unsure. Synonyms: *irresolute, vacillating*

Indemnify compensate for harm or loss

Indifferent unconcerned. Synonyms: *apathetic, dispassionate, nonchalant*

Indignant angry or resentful about unfair treatment. Synonym: *piqued*

Indulgence a pleasure that one allows oneself

Industriously with focused hard work in mind. Synonyms for industrious: *assiduous, conscientious, diligent, sedulous*

Inept clumsy, incompetent. Antonym: *adroit*

Inexplicable not explainable

Infidelity unfaithfulness

Infinitesimally an extremely small amount

Insidious gradually progressing to harmful consequences

Insolent rudely or arrogantly disrespectful. Synonyms: *audacious, cheeky, impertinent, impudent, sassy*

Jubilant very happy, triumphant

Judicial of a court, relating to judgment

Lancet a small surgical knife with a sharp point

Literally factually, exactly

Lithe flexible and graceful. Synonyms: *agile, lissome, nimble, supple*

Livid really, really mad. Synonyms: *incensed, infuriated, irate*

Loathes hates. Synonyms for loathe: *abhor, detest, disdain, scorn*

Lumbered walked in a slow, awkward manner

Make amends make up for, compensate. Synonyms: *atone, expiate, indemnify, redress*

Malice ill will. Synonym: *malevolence*

Mandatory required. Synonyms: *compulsory, obligatory, requisite*

Martyred showing a look of exaggerated discomfort to evoke sympathy, killed for one's views

Maternally related to or like a mother, on your mother's side

Mechanically automatically, without thinking

Melancholy sad

Menace threat

Mercifully with mercy, fortunately

Micro small

Miffed annoyed. Synonyms: *irked, peeved*

Misogynistic hating women

Modulate regulate, change the tone of

Monochromes pictures in shades of one color

Monopolizing having the largest portion of

Monotonous only one sound, lacking in variety

Morbid gloomy and disturbing. Synonyms: *macabre, morose*

Morosely gloomily

Mortal deadly or fatal

Mortality death. Synonym for mortal: *transient*

Muddled confused. Synonym: *befuddled*

Multifarious many and varied

Multihued many colored

Mused said while reflecting (thinking)

Muted quiet, softened. Synonym: *subdued*

Myopic shortsighted

Myriad many, a countless number. Synonyms: *innumerable, multifarious, multiplicity, plethora*

Nape back of the neck

Niche a comfortable or appropriate position

Noble dignified, honorable

Nocturnes musical compositions about the night

Nonchalant casual and calm, uninterested. Synonyms: *dispassionate, indifferent*

Nostalgically longingly remembering the past. Synonym: *wistfully*

Novelty a new and unfamiliar thing

Oblivious totally unaware. Antonym: *vigilant*

Obstinate stubborn. Synonyms: *intractable, obdurate, pertinacious, recalcitrant, tenacious*

Obstreperous noisy and unruly

Ocher brownish-yellow

Offhand casual and possibly rude. Synonyms: *brusque, cavalier, flippant, tactless*

Ogle stare with excessive or possibly offensive sexual desire

Ominous threatening. Synonyms: *foreboding, inauspicious, menacing*

Omnipresent present in all places, common. Synonym: *ubiquitous*

Opaque solid, unclear, or not transparent; a difficult or unclear concept that is hard to grasp

Ostentatious over the top display of wealth. Synonyms: *pretentious, showy*

Palliate relieve, but not cure

Pallid pale

Pariah outcast

Pathetic pitiful

Patronizing kind but with a superior attitude, supporting, or being a customer. Synonyms: *condescending, demeaning, denigrating*

Peripheral at the edge

Permanence lastingness, the state of remaining the same. Synonyms: *eternalness, intransience*

Permeable allowing liquids to pass through

Pertinacious stubborn and annoying

Petulance sulky bad-temperedness. Synonym: *peevishness*

Picturesque quaint and pretty

Plagued deeply troubled

Plaits interlaced strands

Plausible reasonable, probable, or believable. Synonyms: *credible, feasible*

Plethora too many

Poignantly evoking bittersweet feelings

Prattled chattered, babbled

Precariously unsteadily. Synonym: *perilously*

Pretense false display. Synonyms: *facade, guise, pretext*

Profusion large amount. Synonyms: *abundance, cornucopia*

Proprietary possessive

Providentially fortunately, with divine intervention. Synonyms for providential: *auspicious, opportune*

Proximity nearness. Synonym: *propinquity*

Prudent sensible, acting with regard for the future

Purgatory a place of misery

Qualify add reservations, make less complete, or gain eligibility. Synonym for qualified: *tempered*

Raucously loudly and harshly. Synonyms for raucous: *clamorous, obstreperous, strident, vociferous*

Recalcitrant stubbornly uncooperative with authority

Recoiled flinched back

Reflexively unconsciously, automatically

Relent stop, surrender.
Synonyms: *abate, capitulate*

Remorseful regretful.
Synonyms: *contrite, penitent,
repentant*

Repentant regretful

Repressing suppressing

Reproachful scolding

Reproving scolding

Resigned accepting defeat or
some other undesirable result

Reveling in getting great
enjoyment from

Reverent deeply respectful

Rhetorical asked with no answer
expected, the use of effective
or convincing language (style)

Ruefully regretfully

Ruse trick

Russet reddish-brown

Sagely wisely. Synonyms for
wise: *astute, sagacious, shrewd*

Saturated completely soaked or
drenched. Synonym: *sodden*

Sauntered walked in a slow and
leisurely manner

Scornfully with resentment
or mocking. Synonyms:
*contemptuously, derisively,
disdainfully*

Scrawl messy writing

Scrutinize closely examine

Seldom rarely

Seraphic angelic

Serene calm and peaceful.
Synonyms: *placid, tranquil*

Shambled moved with a slow,
shuffling walk

Shrouded covered

Sinister wicked. Synonyms:
*baleful, depraved, heinous, impious,
iniquitous, malevolent, menacing,
nefarious, pernicious*

Sinuous lithe

Smugly with excessive pride.
Synonyms for smug: *arrogant,
bombastic, haughty, pompous*

Soberly seriously and sincerely.
Synonyms for sober: *solemn,
somber*

Sodden totally soaked.
Synonym: *saturated*

Solemn serious. Synonyms:
grave, sober, somber

Solitary alone. Synonym: *reclusive*

Sparse scattered, small amount of

Stammered stuttered, stumbled
with words

Statuesque attractively tall and
imposing

Sterile totally clean, free of bacteria; uninspiring, unproductive, or unable to produce offspring

Stipulation a requirement

Strident making a loud grating noise

Substandard below the standard

Subtly slightly, indirectly, or in a way that's understated

Sullenly with a gloomy and irritable mood. Synonyms for sullen: *doleful, dour, glum, lugubrious, melancholic, morose, surly*

Superfluous unnecessary, more than needed

Supplement add something that completes

Suppress restrain, prevent. Synonyms: *quell, squelch*

Surly hostile

Surmised guessed, concluded

Surreptitiously secretly. Synonyms: *clandestinely, covertly, furtively*

Sympathetic showing concern or compassion

Tactful full of tact. Synonym: *diplomatic*

Tainted contaminated

Tenacity persistence, stubbornness

Tendrils strands of hair, shoots of a climbing plant

Tenor tone, a singing voice between baritone and alto

Terminator one who terminates or kills

Tersely briefly

Threshold the floor of a doorway

Thwarted prevented. Synonym: *stymied*

Token small, a symbol

Topaz dark golden color, a gemstone

Tousled messy (usually for hair)

Translucent semi-transparent

Tyrant cruel and harsh leader

Unconditional total, subject to no conditions. Synonyms: *absolute, categorical, unequivocal, unmitigated, unqualified, untempered*

Undulated moved in a flowing wavelike motion

Unequivocally definitely. Synonyms: *indubitably, unambiguously*

Unerringly without making an error, always right

Unscathed unharmed

Urbane courteous and refined

Vacillating wavering between two decisions

Vague unclear, indefinite. Synonyms: *ambiguous, amorphous*

Vain useless. Synonym: *futile*

Veered switched direction suddenly. Synonym: *wheeled*

Vehemently with very strong feeling. Synonyms: *fervently, fervidly*

Veiling covering. Synonym for veil: *shroud*

Veracity truthfulness

Verbose wordy

Verdant green with vegetation

Verified confirmed

Vestiges remaining bits of something disappearing. Synonym: *remnants*

Vile terrible, wicked. Synonyms: *baleful, depraved, heinous, impious, iniquitous, malevolent, menacing, nefarious, pernicious, sinister*

Vitally very, crucially. Synonym for vital: *imperative*

Vituperative bitter and harsh criticism

Vivid lively, bright, or clear

Vociferous loudly shouting

Vogue the popular fashion or style

Warily cautiously. Synonyms: *cagily, circumspectly, vigilantly*

Wheeling turning quickly, moving something in a vehicle that has wheels

Willowy slim and lithe

Wistfully reflectively, longingly. Synonym: *nostalgically*

Woolgathering daydreaming

Wryly with dry humor